Parliament vs. People

Other Books by Philip Resnick

The Land of Cain *(1977)*
Essays in B.C. Political Economy
  (ed. with Paul Knox; 1974)

Parliament vs. People

**An Essay on Democracy
and Canadian
Political Culture**

Philip Resnick

NEW STAR BOOKS • VANCOUVER

First printing September 1984
1   2   3   4   5   88   87   86   85   84

Canadian Cataloguing in Publication Data

Resnick, Philip, 1944—
Parliament vs. people

Bibliography: p.
ISBN 0-919573-30-4 (bound).—ISBN
0-919573-31-2 (pbk.)

1. Canada - Politics and government - Addresses,
essays, lectures. 2. Canada - Economic policy -
Addresses, essays, lectures. 3. Democracy -
Addresses, essays, lectures. I. Title.
JL65.1984 R47 1984   320.971   C84-091393-1

Publication of this book was financially assisted by the Canada Council and by
the Government of British Columbia through the British Columbia Cultural Fund
and Lottery Revenues.

Printed and bound in Canada

New Star Books Ltd.
2504 York Avenue
Vancouver, B.C.
Canada   V6K 1E3

Preface

This essay reflects a number of concerns. First, it engages in a critical discussion of Canadian political culture and the relative absence in this country of a tradition of popular democracy; what we have instead is a hybrid of parliamentarism of the top-down variety and statism. Second, it analyses the procedures by which the new Canadian constitution was acquired in 1982 and tries to suggest what a more democratic style of constitution making might have given us. Third, it asks how we might introduce greater citizen participation into the political structures of nation-states such as Canada. Fourth, it outlines the type of economic arrangements which would be required for a more participatory type of polity to work.

This sounds like a tall order for an essay. And if it were not meant quite deliberately as a foray into speculative, at times even utopian, thought, it might indeed be an irresponsible undertaking. We are not supposed to play too freely with political ideas in this country, nor are we often invited to rethink the principles by which we are governed or economically ruled.

But in an essay, as opposed to a Royal Commission Report or an academic tome, a wide-ranging set of concerns can be raised in a short space. There is no need to footnote every argument or to rebut all possible objections before daring to offer one's opinion. On the contrary, the essay form offers an incentive to present one's arguments, however diverse, as pithily and forcefully as possible.

I have tried to do that in this essay. It is addressed to readers who share my conviction that political ideas are worthy of higher consideration than they receive in English Canada. It is addressed, even more, to those who think Canadian political institutions—the parliamentary system in particular—are not the last word in democratic theory or practice. It is addressed to those on the left who, when envisaging economic alternatives to a corporate-dominated capitalism, may be eager for something different from the familiar nostrum of state ownership.

Let me acknowledge a few debts on this occasion. To UBC, for allowing me a sabbatical year 1982-83, during which, thousands of kilometres from Canada, a first draft of this text was written. To the Social Sciences & Humanities Research Council of Canada for a small research grant that same year which allowed me to probe widely into the shape of socialist argument and democratic theorizing in Western Europe. To a number of close friends, including Frank Cunningham, Danny Drache, Pat Marchak, John Richards and Pauline Vaillancourt, who provided encouragement and helpful comments. To Petula Muller for her help in retyping the manuscript. To Janet Cotgrave of New Star Books for her valuable services as an editor. To Andromache, Amos and Jonah, whose company, both in Volos and Vancouver, helped sustain me through this project.

In keeping to the essay genre, there are no footnotes in the text. I have, however, appended a short bibliography with references to some of the themes covered.

P.R.
Vancouver, 1984

I
Parliamentary vs. Popular Sovereignty

In the modern world many states claim to be democracies.
The Soviet Union and its allies refer to themselves as
socialist or "people's democracies." Western states,
whether presidential or parliamentary in character, refer to
themselves as liberal democracies. And in the third world
there are numerous regimes—whether one party,
multi-party, or no-party in character—which call themselves democratic.

The purpose of this essay is not to sift through these
competing claims, let alone to take the defence of any one
model against all comers. In my eyes, none of these states
lives up to a working model of democracy, defined as
power in the hands of the people, while most actively
militate against this.

My particular concern is Canada. I will argue that
Canada, far from being a beacon to others, as pompous
politicians or editorial writers occasionally argue, has a
long way to go before beginning to approximate a genuine
democracy. Let me not be misunderstood. In many
respects, Canada is a model liberal state (though it has not
always been so, as a quick recalling of October 1970, the
internment of Japanese Canadians during World War II,

1

the disenfranchisement of many groups into the latter half of this century, the wholesale repression of strikes in the first part of this century, or the inequitable treatment of native people throughout most of Canadian history would suggest). But there is a vast difference between a liberal state and a democratic one. This lies at the root of my critique of Canadian political culture.

Canada has recently been through an experience—the patriation and recasting of its constitution—which should have been cause for celebration. In most other countries, liberal or not, a constitution is the basic document by which the polity is governed. Drafting a constitution is a historic event, surrounded with much political debate and interest. Many countries have drafted constitutions as a direct result of revolution, war or decolonization. In such circumstances, it is seen as a privileged moment in the life of a people. In other cases, constitution writing has followed on some significant change of regime: from dictatorship to constitutional government (in Greece, Spain and Portugal in the 1970s); from military rule to civilian or vice versa; from parliamentary to presidential. These also constitute important historical moments but the degree of popular participation may be severely limited, for example, to the ratification of the text through a referendum in which free and open debate may be prohibited.

But what is one to make of a country which, in the midst of neither a crisis (unless one chooses to glorify the 1980 Quebec referendum with this overworked term) nor a massive change in political direction, engages in a constitutional exercise where the political leaders essentially work out the parameters of the new framework behind closed doors? True, these leaders held office as a result of elections in which the people of Canada as a whole, or in the various provinces, vote. But in no case were they elected with a mandate to engage in constitution making.

2

During the year and a half that the process dragged on they were not interested in fostering widespread public discussion or participation. Nor, in the end, did they feel any compulsion to refer their collective work (collective with the significant dissent of Quebec) to the people of Canada. It was only fitting, then, that when this revised and patriated constitution was proclaimed in April 1982, it was by the Queen of England in a ceremony on a largely empty Parliament Hill, amid general public indifference.

Why should this have been so? Why did a normally edifying and uplifting experience become, in the Canadian context, a politically demobilizing one? What can we learn about Canadian democracy from the unfolding of these strange events—referendum night promises to Quebec by an ebullient federal Prime Minister, first ministers' conferences preceded by weeks of high-level negotiations among civil servants and ministers, leaked documents, parliamentary hearings, meetings among the Premiers, judicial appeals, and a whole new round of federal-provincial negotiations culminating in the November 1981 agreement. What does this suggest about our underlying political culture?

It is here that we discover a disquieting thread running through Canadian history. What we have just been through is not that different from the events of 1864-67. Then, too, colonial politicians, with no explicit mandate from their constituents, drafted what was to become the British North America Act (which survives as the substantive part of the new constitution). That document as well was never referred to the electorates of the colonies. Indeed, skulduggery was practiced in New Brunswick by Canadian and British politicians to assure the return of a pro-Confederation Premier after an 1865 election had gone the other way. It would appear that constitution making over the heads of the people is a Canadian political tradition.

This is not the only archaism underpinning Canadian political culture. The opening of the original B.N.A. Act speaks of "Victoria, by the Grace of God, Queen, with the consent of the Lords, Spiritual and Temporal, and Commons," enacting what, in other jurisdictions, is more correctly attributed to the people. "We the people" reads the opening passage of the American Constitution. Popular sovereignty is the constant refrain of the Declaration of the Rights of Man and of the Citizen and of the various pronouncements of the assemblies and conventions during the French Revolution. Sovereignty is vested directly in the people in these systems. In the B.N.A. Act, however, sovereign power resides in Monarch-in-Parliament. Nothing in our newly patriated constitution alters this original delineation.

This constitution, I shall argue later, is wholly inadequate to the needs of a country in the late 20th century. But for the moment I wish to say a little more about the implications of grounding sovereignty not in the people directly, but in a set of institutions—partly elective and partly not.

The Queen-in-Parliament formula comes to us from a long history of constitutional development in England and Great Britain. Through the centuries, the knights and squires represented in the two houses of the English Parliament advanced claims for consultation on all matters of public finance, and by extension on all other matters in the public domain. Though the origins of Parliament were feudal, the institution survived the transition of the War of the Roses and Tudor absolutism to emerge as a powerful political force in 17th-century England. While in no sense a popular body—only a tiny percentage of the male population was enfranchised and the Lords was, by definition, a non-elected house—Parliament did articulate a programme of liberal rights in opposition to the Stuarts.

4

The Petition of Right of 1628 was one expression of this. Widespread demands for freedom of conscience in religious and other matters were another expression throughout the civil war years. This war, as we know, culminated in the triumph of the Parliamentary Armies and the execution of the king. But the Parliamentary side was less than united. The traditional political elites who dominated the Long Parliament which sat from 1640-53 were not interested in institutional reforms, and were increasingly wary of the power of the army. Cromwell and his generals, for their part, had not engaged in bloody war to see their own power frittered away by an Assembly unrepresentative of what they took to be the live currents of English society. While from below—from within the rank-and-file of the army and outside it and from the Levellers and the Diggers—one began to hear voices demanding the democratization of the political system: broadening of the suffrage and greater economic equality.

These last-mentioned reforms were not adopted until the 19th and 20th centuries—and then only partially. But the institution of parliament survived the Restoration of 1660 and emerged strengthened from the forced flight of James II and the calling to the throne of William and Mary in 1688. The Bill of Rights of 1689 solemnized the powers of monarch and Parliament. It was no less eloquent in its comparative silence regarding the rights of the people.

This should not surprise us. There was little place for democracy in the liberal theory of the 17th and 18th centuries. The relevant political class in England consisted of the large estate owners, the better-off gentry, and a number of the richer merchants of London or Bristol thrown in for good measure. Agricultural labourers, artisans, weavers, joiners and the rest were simply not considered capable of political participation. And this was certainly the prevailing Whig attitude toward the industrial working class when it began to emerge in the second half of the 18th century.

Liberal theory was chiefly concerned with limiting the power of kings, a goal which could best be secured through the separation of powers, endowing the legislature and the judiciary with rights which were safe from executive encroachment. Thus, Parliament would be convened at least once a year. It would vote all legislative enactments and would further have the right to impeach ministerial officials. Its proceedings would be free and unhindered, as had not been true during the Stuart years, and Parliament would control the power of the purse. With time this was extended to the larger sphere of executive action, with the doctrine of ministerial responsibility to Parliament.

If "the people" existed for such theorists as Locke or Montesquieu, Bolingbroke or Madison, they represented more of a potential threat to a liberal order than a bulwark to it. Locke did not hesitate to place property first and foremost among the values of civil society and to oppose any threats which might arise to it. Montesquieu was candid about his opposition to democracy, speaking about the ineptitude of the lower classes for the art of government. As for Madison, several of his contributions to *The Federalist Papers* emphasized the dangers to liberty which, in a republican scheme of government, were likely to come from the people.

England was more successful than 18th-century America or France in fending off the doctrine of popular sovereignty. While the revolutions in the latter two countries did not go much beyond liberal forms, a democratic quality was inherent to both. In the American Revolution, the more conservative of the two, this took the form of demands for a clearly enunciated bill of rights, for broad participation in the framing of the constitution, and for something close to universal white male suffrage in the elections of President and Congress. While these demands were not fully met—only some states elected constitutional

6

conventions and delegates, and the President and Senate were elected indirectly according to the original constitution—they represented a democratic sentiment which was to flower during the Jeffersonian and Jacksonian presidencies and beyond.

In France, Rousseau had articulated a theory of popular sovereignty in his discussion of the general will in *The Social Contract*. While Rousseau reserved democracy for the legislative rather than the executive realm, he underlined the inalienability of popular sovereignty. He berated the English for their faith in septennially elected Parliaments, emphasizing the importance of direct citizen participation in political affairs. It was the people, assembled annually, who should decide whether the existing constitution was to be kept or altered.

Rousseau was, of course, only one intellectual influence on the French Revolution. Still, from the initial events of 1789 through the stormy days of the Convention and the Jacobin dictatorship, one can trace an emerging doctrine of popular sovereignty. This concept was not without difficulties. Who could be said to embody it—elected representatives or the people themselves? If the latter, could the active members of the Parisian *sections* or the participants in some of the more memorable *journees* be identified with the whole of the French people? Or could Robespierre and St. Just claim to embody that popular will, even through the darkest days of the Terror?

I do not propose to tackle here the implications of these widely diverging interpretations of popular sovereignty. (One need only think of the Russian Revolution to see some of the analogies and difficulties). But let us be clear about what was displaced by popular sovereignty. It swept away the skein of feudal privilege, undid the not-so-sacred powers of the king, and allowed to the third estate and, marginally, to *le petit peuple*, a first taste of political participation. In other words, with one stroke it abolished

7

aristocratic pretensions and legitimist claims to absolute power. No wonder that, contradiction of contradictions, in Tsarist Russia and Junker Prussia the more enlightened officials and philosophers toasted the fall of the Bastille. A new political concept had been born, which was to sweep first Europe, then the world.

But not England. And not those parts of the British Empire most beholden to the old imperial power. The ruling class of England would have nothing to do with the new, continental concept of sovereignty. Indeed, not only was England soon at war with revolutionary France, but repression of the severest kind rained down on those who dared to sympathize with the revolution's idea. Priestly's house was burnt, dissenting newspapers and publications shut down, and every effort made to ensure the contagion did not spread to the popular classes of the land. For over three decades, Britain endured one of the most reactionary governments in its history, with those most intellectually alive, such as Shelley and Byron, forced to flee abroad for air.

This is not to belabour the English reaction to the French Revolution. It is simply to point out that much of England's hostility stemmed from a concept of sovereignty which looked to an unreformed Parliament and doting monarch as the ramparts against change. When Burke thundered uncompromising hostility toward those who announced new experiments in the political order of things, he spoke for the British political class for whom the social contract linked the living with the dead, the present with the venerable past. The British Constitution, grounded in King and Parliament, must never depart from its origin.

This rather dark constitutional doctrine is part of what, in more recent times, Perry Anderson and Tom Nairn have come to indict and E.P. Thompson to celebrate as "the peculiarities of the English." The doctrine assumed special

8

virtue in haphazard historical development and eternal merit in institutions grounded in a particular time and place. It assumed, in its extreme forms, an exceptionalism for the English, who had nothing to learn from the experience of others.

The British parliamentary tradition, needless to say, was not entirely evil; through successive reforms the system became more open to the middle and working classes. Yet the stuffiness and aristocratic character of the old parliamentary system carried over into the new and was transposed in turn to the colonies. There it became the formula for an obtuseness and colonial-mindedness that long blocked the development of a vital political culture. In a two-nation society such as Canada, with a large infusion of immigrants, British exceptionalism and parliamentary fetishism easily become impediments to democracy. They excluded the political experience of the United States, France or other European countries as "un-British" and therefore "un-Canadian," and thus wrote off as illegitimate any concept of popular, as opposed to parliamentary, sovereignty. This is the direct legacy of the monopoly which the British Constitution came to hold as the fountainhead of political wisdom for English-speaking Canadians.

II
The Legacy of Counter-revolution

In most textbooks of Canadian history, the achievement of representative government is hailed as a high point in our political emancipation. Before Baldwin, Lafontaine and Elgin lay the dark ages of colonial rule. Thereafter, the course was set for 1867 and beyond.

This is a convenient reading of history if you assume parliamentary institutions to be the epitome of democratic practice. It is convincing if you can skate over the political conflicts and economic divisions which had preceded the emergence of this new representative system. For the ideologues of Canadian political culture, Whig or Tory, the 1840s are the era of new beginnings. But it would be more accurate to speak of an *ersatz* beginning, an attempt to cover up the failure of the popular revolts of the 1830s.

It is essential to recall the 1830s to understand the nature of what followed. Of course, one could press the enquiry further back, to the Conquest on the French side or the earlier nature of the *ancien regime* as it was experienced in New France, to the coming of the Loyalists and the atavistic streak they brought to their new country. But this would take us too far afield. It would, moreover, lead away from the real turning point in our history.

10

We have not done justice to the crushing of the 1837 rebellions. We who live in a century where revolution and counter-revolution are the stuff of world politics can surely recognize the significance that such events have. We should therefore assess what the failure of revolution entailed for our own body politic.

I do not want to romanticize what the rebellions in Upper and Lower Canada stood for. Each hoped for representative institutions to replace the oligarchical forces crystallized around English governors. Both rebellions saw the path to emancipation in a break with the British colonial system. Both were inspired by republican ideals current in the United States and France, and both should be seen as national liberation movements in embryonic form. This was undoubtedly more manifest in Lower Canada, where Papineau and his Patriotes saw in English rule something ethnically alien to the majority of the colony's population. But even in Upper Canada, the Reformers were prepared to sever the links with Britain once and for all to achieve a more just political and economic order.

If these rebellions had succeeded, if we were able to speak of the Canadian or the Quebec Revolution(s) of 1837, what would have been different? It seems futile, I know, to play at historical might-have-beens. But I also know how high a price we are paying for having ignored such historical alternatives. Our new constitution makers counted on such ignorance in their recent hijacking of the democratic process.

A Canadian revolution in the 1830s would have opened the door to one of several possibilities: absorption of the fledgling colonies into the USA; the emergence of separate republics in the northern part of this continent with some kind of weak link among them; or the emergence of a federation among these ex-colonies, but of a type more democratic than occurred in 1867.

11

While most critics of the rebellions assume that absorption into the USA was inevitable, I am not so sure. One can argue that the economics of the old staple trade—fur and timber—which had differentiated Canada from the United States during the periods of British and French rule would have continued to militate against absorption into the United States. One can point to the independence of much of Latin America from Spain during the same period, without these colonies falling prey to American annexation. (Though it is true that Mexico, in particular, lost much land to a westward-expanding United States.) Nor is it clear that either the Loyalists of Upper Canada or the French Canadians of Lower would have wanted to become full-fledged members of the American union.

Why can we not imagine a Canadian revolution, much like the Belgian separation from the Netherlands in 1830, producing an integrally Canadian arrangement? A loose arrangement would have been possible in the late 1830s. There might have been an association between Upper and Lower Canada, including perhaps the Maritimes. This could have resembled, at best, the confederal arrangements among the thirteen colonies after the American Revolution before the establishment of the United States. Such an arrangement would, doubtlessly, have proven economically ineffective and militarily puny when compared to the United States. The pressures for a tighter union to forestall annexation would then have grown, especially as the United States moved relentlessly toward the Pacific.

I am not certain what would have become of the Prairies and British Columbia under these conditions, especially with the British military presence removed. Perhaps these would have met the fate of Texas, New Mexico and California. But it is also possible that a Canadian Union in the 1840s or 1850s could have secured them for Canada, especially if this Union pursued a dynamic and enlightened settlement policy.

What kind of Union might this have been? It probably would have had more of the attributes of the Swiss Confederation, with a good deal of reserve powers residing with the provinces. We can further imagine a constitution emerging from formal discussion among the representatives of the ex-colonies, with electoral ratification to secure it. As a mercantile society with a largely agrarian population, a post-revolutionary Canada would have fostered a liberal state, possibly a cross between American presidential and English parliamentary in form. So far, at least, we do not seem to be far removed from the history which we know.

One crucial ingredient would have been present, however, that was absent in the process leading up to 1867: direct popular involvement. Successful revolution in the late 1830s would have made the farmers and burghers, the artisans and labourers who had overthrown the Family Compact, direct participants in forging their own history. It would have entailed, as revolutions have elsewhere, a politicization that we rarely experience and seldom imagine in this country. The involvement of those who had so recently fought for their own liberation could not have been cavalierly swept aside by whichever politicians now came to the fore.

A democratic tradition would have taken root. A concept of popular sovereignty would have been built into the foundation of our constitution, a bill of rights that makes clear the limitations, as well as the powers, of the state. And, best of all, we would have an example of direct participation to counterpose to the claims of legislature or executive, Parliament or Cabinet, to a monopoly of political power.

Things might have gone differently. The ex-colonies might have gone separate ways, or the American eagle swooped down and taken large chunks of what we today call Canada. I cannot disprove this. But I think my version is no less plausible and the type of Canada that would have emerged in such a scenario would have been less a colonial hybrid than what we ended up with. We would not have Quebec as the permanent hostage to defeat; rather it would have become a willing, though exacting, member of a popularly agreed-upon federation. We would not have had the arrogance of the old English elites, embedded in British practice and tradition, but a more popular form of government. Instead of monarchs and Governors-General on the English Canadian side, and an ultra-Montane Church at war with the modern world on the French, we might just have gotten that mixture of republican sentiment and revolutionary *virtu* out of which a democratic ethos can develop.

The point of this excercize is not to remake history. It is to underline, by contrasting a possible alternative, the nature of the road we travelled down. That road was neither revolutionary nor republican. It also, in my opinion, was not democratic.

The events of the 1840s and 1860s were an indirect response by our governing elites to the failure of revolution. In the wake of the Durham Report, political reform was on the agenda. If representative government could secure Canada for the Empire, well and good. But first, Lower Canada was punished by being forced into an unequal union with Upper. The democratic forces were harrassed with the exile of their leaders, while the landed and mercantile forces in the politics of the colonies were reinforced. When reform came in 1848 it was from above, not below, as a grant from imperial power. Liberal institutions were simply grafted onto what was essentially the old colonial superstructure. British peers, masquerading as governors, still wielded important power, for authority flowed constitutionally from the Crown. The politicians knew that the key to political change lay in London, not in popular struggles at home.

Seen from this vantage point, the achievement of responsible government is notably diminished. Canadian history ends before it can begin. And in its beginnings are the half-measures and petty compromises which it still exhibits. Instead of the Patriotes and the Reformers we have Baldwin and Lafontaine, followed by Macdonald and Cartier, Laurier, Borden, Mackenzie King and all their postwar progeny. We have the Grand Trunk Railway allied with London financiers, followed by the CPR and Bank of Montreal, and the 20th-century entente between Canadian resources and American capital.

We have a country in which French Canadians are never entirely at home, where they must fall back on an institution like the Church, whose role expands to fill the ideological vacuum left by the crushing of the revolt. Would Bourget, Lafleche and other reactionary clerics have had it as easy in a Quebec which had freed itself from the British yoke and set out, possibly in association with English Canada, to master its own future? Would Taschereau and Duplessis have enjoyed such unbridled triumphs?

English-speaking Canadians for their part, could only bask in the reflected glory of the British empire. Oh, the most Orange of Ontario's Loyalists might stand siege with Gordon at Khartoum, ride with Kipling in the hills, and teetotal with Victoria at her Diamond Jubilee. But the rest of Canada's scattered homesteaders and labourers had more immediate and pressing things to do. Nor did the great wave of non-British immigrants into Canada, which began at the turn of the century, find in empires on which suns never set the stuff of nationhood. One needed something different to weld together the northern half of a continent.

That something would not come from the Confederation Debates with their bickering over railway subsidies and public debt, nor from the B.N.A. Act which, after 1867, consecrated the new *status quo*. True, Canada now had a central government, with some division of responsibility between it and the provinces, but there was not a hint in this British North America Act that any citizens' rights existed *independently* of their rulers' desires.

The document, as could be expected, was a constitution for parliamentary politicians. It outlined the powers of the Governor-General, the Senate and the Commons, discussed the taxing and general powers of the various levels of government, and left everything else for time and jurisprudence to resolve. Not only was there no founding democratic myth, but the people were asked to take seats up in the stalls while their betters got on with the business of serious law making. And in the stalls they remained.

When Canadians are called upon to celebrate Dominion Day, Canada Day or whatever label one affixes to July 1st, enthusiasm is hard to muster. It was not, after all, their decision which united the colonies. Nor were they consulted about the terms or even the date of Confederation. The Proclamation came from London, and did little more than transfer from one Parliament to another, still under the British sovereign, a package of legal and political rights. These were not individual rights, or even collective rights, expressed in popular language. They did not speak the language of the Rights of Man or of life, liberty, and the pursuit of happiness. It is hard to get excited about the handiwork of railway buccaneers and their kept lawyers.

Such is Canadian history. Some try to prettify things: downplay the residual powers of the Crown; fob off the property clause (Section 23) which ensured only the wealthy would be Senators; suggest that the Commons is the true custodian of democratic liberties—it doesn't wash. You cannot make history without direct participa-

16

tion of the people and call it democracy. 1867 was made over our heads. It was the fruit of the smashed hopes of 1837-38. The B.N.A. Act was the constitutional document of the Canadian counter-revolution.

III
Peace, Order and Good Government

"Peace, order and good government" is what Section 91 of the B.N.A. Act claimed our parliamentary system is about. And the bill of particulars which followed fleshed out this conception in more prosaic fashion.

Some might wish to argue the innocent intention of the phrase, which does little more than pinpoint what many liberal states claim to provide. Surely, they would argue, "war, disorder and bad government" would not make an appealing formula for a political system. And they would be right if the choice were so limited.

Others have argued the Hobbesian quality of this passage, evoking the celebrated *Leviathan*. *Leviathan* drew lessons from the English Civil War of the 1640s and it elevated peace under a single sovereign, be it king or parliament, to be the highest good. This is a tempting analogy, particularly if we follow C.B. Macpherson's interpretation of Hobbes as a nondemocratic liberal writer who sought to reconcile the needs of market society with an authoritative political power. But it is not certain that Hobbes was attempting only this in his work, nor does it follow that the Fathers of Confederation were writing from the searing experience of civil war which had led

18

Hobbes to vindicate undivided sovereignty. True, the United States was torn by civil war in the early 1860s and this weighed on our politicians in determining the balance between federal and provincial power. But it is unlikely that this concern was the determining feature of their constitutional thought.

I contend that the above phrase is neither innocent nor Hobbesian. Rather, in a peculiarly Canadian way, it captures the essence of our counter-revolutionary tradition. It is not innocent because there were other historical alternatives, not least the formulations which resulted from the two great revolutions of the preceding century. Each of these placed liberty at the centre of a powerful founding myth. It is not Hobbesian because Hobbes was too radical a theorist for the Victorian stomachs of our Confederation elites. *Leviathan* reduced politics to a series of psychological drives and deduced from this the need for a single commanding power. This was not the stuff that Macdonald, Cartier, or Tupper were likely to adopt. It is not evident, moreover, that these gentlemen—unlike Madison, Adams and Jefferson or Mirabeau, Condorcet and Robespierre—lost much sleep reading the political theorists of the past. The judicial perorations of Blackstone and other epigones of the common law were, for them, an adequate substitute.

What our Founding Fathers were doing was consolidating an orderly, as opposed to disorderly, move from direct colonial rule to Home Rule. They were not trying to set out grand principles of government, nor was their goal to justify *any* kind of order. They had a particular kind of order in mind, the parliamentary system as it had evolved in Britain, combining the interests of monarch, lords and commons. If by the latter part of the 19th century this system was increasingly responsive to the wishes of an electorate, restricted or enlarged, it was by no means a servant of the electorate. The members of the two houses, one appointed, one elected, retained considerable discretion and final say on what would or would not be.

Our constitution makers did not want what they saw as the tempestuous currents of popular democracy, which had wreaked such damage on revolutionary France and the United States, set loose on the good colonies of the north. They wanted something quieter, more discrete, good for the merchant and for the banker, for the lawyer and, perhaps, for the farmer, but not likely to go to anyone's head. The brief experience of the 1830s was enough—we were innoculated against any further outbreaks of the disease.

Parliamentary government, then, was not meant to engage the citizenry in political affairs. It was not to function, as Pericles in his Funeral Oration had claimed for Athens, as a school for democracy. Nor were citizens who placed their private interests over public affairs to be disdained, as in that city-state. Quite the contrary. The assumption was that, aside from voting, the electorate would allow the party politicians to get on with the job which had been so tersely defined as "peace, order and good government." The same assumption held good at the provincial level, confined though it was to matters of "a merely local or private nature." Nowhere in the B.N.A. Act do the Canadian people appear as political subjects in their own right.

It was a conscious omission, reflecting the world view of our Confederation elites. Neither the United States nor France could dispense quite as easily with popular sovereignty. There existed in those countries a reservoir of popularly articulated democracy which could boil over and, with legitimacy, appeal to the revolutionary past. Agrarian and populist ferment, movements for the recall and for popular initiative, were examples of this in the United States. The revolutions of 1830 and 1848, and the proclamation of the Paris Commune in 1871, showed how

20

alive this spirit was in France.

This is not to suggest that there would never be grassroots democratic movements in Canada. Agrarian sentiment in Western Canada at the end of the 19th century and beginning of the 20th was strongly populist. Socialist currents emerged from the working class and had some influence on later government policies. The dominant tradition, however, remained steadfastly elitist and profoundly suspicious of politics from below. The political history of post-1867 Canada reveals the encapsulation of democracy within a parliamentary straitjacket.

What is equally important is the capitalist nature of this harness. Our Senate, House of Commons and Governors-General were not above the economic fray; our governments, federal and provincial, were not neutral vis-a-vis the social and class forces that emerged. If our Governors-General for the first 80 years were scions of British aristocracy, our legislators and Cabinets were more middle class or bourgeois. Yet only a minority were artisans or farmers, and only the tiniest handful were ever workers. With this class background came the policies which fostered a capitalist mode of accumulation. In the mid-19th century Allan McNab summarized it succinctly with his boast, "Railways are my politics."

If I were content with a form of vulgar Marxism, I would reiterate the claim which goes back to Gustavus Myers, that Canadian history is simply a saga of misbegotten wealth. In the machinations of the Baring Brothers (the London bond financiers of the pre-Confederation colonies) and of the Canadian Pacific Railway, I would find the real stuff of Canadian politics. Macdonald, Mackenzie and their provincial counterparts would be but their foils.

Such a view is too simplistic, even though public finance was in many respects central to Confederation politics. I

21

would prefer to argue that we got a carefully circumscribed liberal state in this country, able to finance certain projects like the railway through land and cash grants and the like, but with only limited autonomy vis-a-vis the financiers and capitalists who came to dominate our political economy. What I want to dwell on is the peculiar nature of the parliamentary institutions which we imported and how they helped to legitimize the development of Canadian capitalism.

We tend to forget that the expansion of the franchise that writers like James Mill, John Stuart Mill or Leslie Stephens supported, and politicians like Disraeli or Gladstone introduced, was a response to the pressures of industrial capitalism. The Reform Bills of 1832, 1867 or 1884 in England and similar moves toward universal male suffrage in France under the Second and Third Republics, and in Germany after 1871 were not disinterested attempts to democratize representative institutions for democracy's sake. They were attempts to integrate classes potentially hostile to the political order into that order on terms that the ruling class set. The pre-capitalist foundations of parliaments were retained in upper houses, usually of a hereditary character, while lower houses continued well into the 20th century to be dominated by parties of the bourgeoisie or petty bourgeoisie. The operation of parliamentary institutions was essentially a bourgeois, gentlemanly game, while the extension of the franchise channelled working class demands into this arena as opposed to an extra-parliamentary one. Representation was an alternative to revolutionary activities (such as the working class insurrection in Paris of June 1848 or the Commune of 1871); it was a means to woo the working class and to reassure the middle and ruling classes that any impulse for reform would not run out of bounds.

In North America, universal male franchise was achieved more easily than in Europe. In the United States, white male suffrage had been built into the operation of most state governments and the House of Representatives, with an indirect form of popular franchise deciding the presidency and the membership of the Senate. The lack of feudal tradition, the legacy of the Revolution, and the dynamism of American capitalism made representative institutions seem to be almost natural phenomena. So, at least, they appeared to observers like Alexis de Tocqueville in the 1830s, who saw the United States foreshadowing the path which Europe would ineluctably follow.

When we consider the genesis of our own parliamentary institutions we do well to remember this past. Here, as in the United States, representative institutions and a liberal state corresponded better to an emerging capitalist order, one with widespread freehold ownership of the land, than any European autocracy could have done. Even Orangeman and Loyalists could recognize this. At the same time, British-style parliamentary institutions socialized Canadians to a conservative definition of the public good, one in which the legitimacy of property (both land and capital) could not be easily challenged. With our second-hand parliamentary institutions from England, we inherited a good deal more: an unelected upper house, aristocratic pretensions and parliamentary rituals, royal perogative and, finally, property rights written into the fabric of political culture.

Parliamentarism and capitalism thus went hand in hand. The parties which came to dominate Canadian political life represented different versions of the same economic credo. No wonder Andre Siegfried devoted one of the earliest studies of Canadian politics to "the race question in Canada," not to the social or class questions which were becoming all-important in European politics. So natural was the fusion between railway construction, resource exploitation and "national policy" in the Canadian equation, that they constituted the parliamentary agenda

23

for a half-century and more.

The kind of capitalism which Canada developed was largely dependent on outside forces. This should tell us something further about the derivative character of our political institutions. Canada's place in the international capitalist order was as an exporter of resources and importer of capital and manufactured goods. True, there was a sort of indigenous Canadian capitalism, both in the financial and in certain industrial sectors. And development based on staples or resources was not necessarily a wrong course to pursue for a country with the mix between land and population that Canada had. But Canada was a peripheral power in the capitalist scheme of things, clearly subordinated to the circuits of capital represented by London or New York.

The parliamentary system established in 1867 helped to channel this peripheral capitalist development. The jurisdiction of Canadian parliaments, while large in the domestic economic arena, was small by international standards, and but a pale shadow of the "Mother of Parliaments" in Westminster. Imperial Parliaments and Cabinets administered a vast empire and oversaw foreign and military policy. They retained important reserve powers over Dominion Parliaments and governments, even as London's financial houses retained a tutelary power over our railways and commercial and industrial enterprises. The symbolism of the monarchy continued to lend an unmistakably British flavour to all our national institutions, from Mounted Police to Armed Forces, from currency to postage stamps.

It follows that parliamentary sovereignty was itself something of a myth in 1867, though a potent one that served important ends. It helped validate to the population the "responsible" character of the governing institutions, yet ensured that, through the party system, the interests of indigenous and foreign capital were powerfully represented within the corridors of power. While nothing could *formally* prevent challenges from farmers or working class movements to aspects of governmental policies, the likelihood of them shaping the federal House of Commons and Senate to their own interests was slight. Parliamentary sovereignty fostered attitudes in the population which were nominally participatory but maximally deferential toward those exercizing political power. The mystique of British Crown and Constitution helped make illegitimate *all* forms of political activity not sanctioned or channeled through parliamentary institutions. Finally, parliamentary government defined Canada's status in the international system as a colony that had achieved home rule, thereby encouraging a wider network of trade and financial relationships.

Sovereignty in Monarch-cum-Parliament thus fell a good deal short of a founding democratic myth. It translated faithfully the situation of a late 19th-century society which had neither shed its colonial status nor gone the road of popular struggle to achieve its nationhood. Economic prosperity might follow, but it was coloured by continuing dependency, first on Great Britain then on the United States. A branch-plant parliamentary system was an appropriate symbol of our place in the world economy of capitalism.

IV
The 20th-Century Pattern

What actual difference did the lack of popular sovereignty make to Canadian political culture? If we look at events in 20th-century Canadian history, are we justified in emphasizing this missing strand? Is counter-revolution a latent feature in our politics, and is democratic practice stunted by our parliamentary framework?

Let us examine a few important developments and see whether they can enlighten us in our search.

1. Naval Bills and the entry into World War I
2. Working class radicalism and the Winnipeg General Strike
3. Constitutional developments down to the Statute of Westminster
4. The Great Depression and governmental response
5. World War II and the forging of a North American alliance
6. The coming of the Cold War
7. Quebec nationalism and the federal response
8. The politics of Canadian nationalism

I would not want to suggest that this list is in any way

exhaustive. But it provides an empirical backdrop for our discussion.

1) The controversy that surrounded Canadian support for the British Navy in the period leading up to World War I was a classic illustration of the branch-plant character of our parliamentary system. Just as the most British-inclined elements of English Canada had rallied to the support of the mother country during the Boer War, they now beat the drums for the Imperial Navy in its competition with Germany. The assumption of our native imperialists was that Canadian and British strategic interests were one and the same. It behooved a junior member of the empire to give of itself unstintingly when the senior member called.

1867 had not marked a decisive break with Britain; we were now drawn inextricably into Britain's European conflicts. Nationalist opinion in French Canada— Langevin, Henri Bourassa and others—might object. The new settlers in the West might have different priorities. But dreadnoughts were voted and, in the decisive hours of August 1914, a vote in the British Parliament put Canada at war.

Obviously, there was widespread support in English Canada for these actions. Entry into the war could not have been imposed on a hostile public. But the decision, in any event, was not in the hands of the Canadian people—sovereignty rested with the *British* Parliament.

2) At the end of World War I a wave of political and industrial unrest swept the world. Russia had undergone revolution in 1917; Hungary and Germany threatened to follow suit. In the West, workers organized factory occupations and strikes, helped swell the membership lists of unions, and demanded from their governments and capitalist classes some of the fruits of the victory so bloodily secured.

The Allies may have used the slogan: "Making the World Safe for Democracy." The Versailles Conference was more concerned with dividing up the spoils and making the world safe for capitalism. England and France enhanced their empires at Germany's expense, while the western powers prepared to intervene in Russia on the side of the Whites.

Canada, which was to have a seat in its own name in the new League of Nations, proved no laggard in the Allies' new crusade. A Canadian expeditionary force joined the British at Archangel to help them prop up a doomed cause. Back at home, Borden, Meighen and their supporters fought a more successful battle against the workers of Winnipeg.

There is little reason to believe that the Winnipeg General Strike was meant to be the opening round of a Canadian Bolshevik Revolution. On this much, most historians concur. But the strike signalled a more militant form of working class politics, coming as it did in the aftermath of declining living standards for Canadian workers and extensive war-profiteering by capitalists. The One Big Union, formed in Calgary in February 1919, marked the emergence of a syndicalist form of unionism in Western Canada.

The strike to support Winnipeg's metalworkers was almost universally upheld by the city's working class. The city ground to a halt while a Strike Committee oversaw distribution of certain essential supplies. The Winnipeg business class and its Tory allies in Ottawa responded with systematic repression. Special constables were sworn in, militia transported to the city, as the Committee of 1000, mostly businessmen, began to coordinate the crushing of the strike. Demonstrations were prohibited, strikers shot down in cold blood, working class publications stopped, and key working class leaders interned.

The federal government attempted to paint the Winnipeg Strike as a threat to "peace, order and good government." But if this were the case, then it was because tens of thousands of Winnipeg's workers had a very different conception of democracy than did the Union government elected in the somewhat rigged 1917 election. They seemed to believe, heresy of heresies, that Parliament was not the only legitimate arena for political activity, and that workers had the right to advance and defend their demands without permission of their rulers. The troops sent to Winnipeg and the frigate stationed off the coast of British Columbia were meant to bring home the iron fist within the velvet glove of parliamentarism.

By itself, a tradition of popular sovereignty would not necessarily have brought a different outcome in Winnipeg. The United States experienced its Palmer Raids and Red Scares, notwithstanding the provisions of its Bill of Rights. But I would argue that a parliamentary regime is no better guarantor of democratic rights, while our counter-revolutionary tradition strongly coloured the responses of Meighen and his associates at Winnipeg.

3) The B.N.A. Act made no provisions for constitutional amendment—an oversight which would have been inconceivable in a wholly independent state. Instead, we were suppliants to Westminster each and every time a revision was necessary. More telling still, until 1949 the Judicial Committee of the Privy Council in London retained authority over all questions of constitutional interpretation. It gave a more provincially oriented reading to the B.N.A. Act, for example, than Sections 91 and 92 had intended.

I am not particularly committed to a centralized form of government, but it is a remarkable testimony of our underdeveloped traditions of democracy that matters so important were decided by Law Peers of the British House of Lords. I am not sure we should even have entrusted something of this nature to the exclusive jurisdiction of the appointed judges of our own Supreme Court. Surely the people themselves should have their say on the appropriate division of powers between different levels of government. This is not as far-fetched as some might believe. The constitutions of Switzerland and Australia, to name two, provide for referenda on constitutional amendments. The pace of constitutional reform has been slower, no doubt, than many Swiss or Australians might have liked. But the procedure is, at least, strongly democratic.

In Canada, our federal government and Parliament were the instigators of amendments, but the British Parliament had the final say. The Statute of Westminster in 1931 formalized this arrangement, and recognized a consultative role for the provincial governments. In the absence of a doctrine of popular sovereignty, Parliaments, Canadian and British, became the gatekeepers of constitutional change.

4) The Great Depression was the most serious crisis faced by the capitalist system thus far in this century. (The jury is still out on the present crisis.) As factory after factory shut down, as banks went under and the armies of unemployed swelled, political systems came under unprecedented stress. In Weimar Germany, the crash set the stage for the rise of facism with its Mephistophelean bag of tricks: militarization and totalitarianism. In France, the crisis made the left more appealing and led to the Popular Front government of Leon Blum. Among the more important reforms by this government were the 40-hour week and annual month-long holidays for workers. These were enacted following an unprecedented wave of factory occupations in the spring and early summer of 1936. In England, the so-called National Government of 1931 tried to hold back the dikes which threatened an overextended empire and an unreformed capitalist system. Sweeping changes there came only after 1945, in the wake of wartime radicalization and the Labour victory. In the United States, 1933 saw the inauguration of Roosevelt and the start of the New Deal. While less than thorough in its

reform of American capitalism, the New Deal did open the door to social security and a more interventionist state, to greater power for organized labour, and to a whole range of citizen initiatives.

How did Canadian governments respond to the crisis? The answer is: not very well. The Bennett government spent its first four and a half years in office trying to downplay the severity of the Depression. Imperial preferences were established in 1932, to little avail. Expenditures were carefully controlled, while many of the single unemployed were herded into work camps. When some of these objected and organized the On-to-Ottawa Trek of 1935, they were stopped at Regina. Then, in a deathbed conversion to reform in 1935, the Conservatives attempted to introduce bits and pieces of the New Deal into Canada.

The Liberals under King had little more to offer. Bennett's New Deal measures were found to be largely *ultra vires* by the Privy Council, so a Royal Commission was established to look into Dominion-Provincial relations. Social Credit, newly elected in Alberta, sought to interfere with the operations of chartered banks—their legislation was disallowed. Though a number of new or revamped crown corporations like Trans-Canada Airlines, the Bank of Canada or the Wheat Board saw the light of day, the dominant mood at the federal level was of caution.

There was a little more vitality in some provinces, with long-standing party patterns coming unstuck. The 1930s saw the emergence of the CCF and Social Credit, and the Union Nationale in Quebec. But here, too, promises and reality seldom jived. Duplessis, once he had come to power in 1936, quickly betrayed the reform elements of the Action liberale nationale, a major component of his newly formed party. Social Credit moved rapidly from populism of the right to stolid conservative administration. The

CCF, despite initial successes, had only limited impact at the provincial level. Only in Saskatchewan did the CCF actually come to power, and not until 1944.

Overall, in Canada there were fewer political break-throughs and reforms during the Depression than there were elsewhere. While we can be grateful we were spared the politicization of a Nazi Germany, we should ponder whether we did better without a New Deal or a Popular Front. Couldn't grassroots democracy have taken firmer hold, might not the movements of farmers or the unemployed have shaken the political establishment, especially at the centre, more thoroughly? Once more, Canadian political culture revealed itself to be parliamentary, and not popular, in character.

Increased federal power to deal with unemployment was left to the Rowell-Sirois Commission and subsequent federal-provincial conferences to thrash out. Key measures of social security—such as Family Allowances—were hatched by mandarins and Cabinet committees in the cloistered boardrooms of wartime Ottawa. Keynesian measures arrived in Canada not with a bang, but a whimper. Mackenzie King—a colonial, equivocating, insecure and trite figure—came to symbolize our political culture. We got the kind of leader that our history had taught us to expect.

5) Canada's entry into World War II was, at least, formally carried out in its own name. Our declaration of war on Germany followed Britain's by one week. This war, no less than the first, tested Canada's unity—sentiment in Quebec was strongly opposed to overseas conscription. For the first—and last—time in Canadian history, the whole population was actually consulted on a major issue. The 1942 plebiscite did not resolve the conscription question, since English Canada voted overwhelmingly in favour and French-speaking Quebec against. It did, however, represent a fleeting instance of

popular, as opposed to parliamentary, legitimization.

But we should not read too much into it. Mackenzie King was seeking a way out of his earlier anti-conscription promise and the Liberal Cabinet was divided—they really could not ask the Privy Council in London to decide this one too.

More significant for the long term was the strategic reorientation of Canada toward the United States which occurred during the war. This was done in secrecy, beginning with the Ogdensburg meeting between King and Roosevelt in August 1940, and carried on by the Permanent Joint Board of Defence during the war. The Canadian economy became increasingly continental with the integration of the productive capacities of the two countries.

There is no reason to lament the corresponding weakening of our links with Britain; I will leave George Grant and other Tory balladeers to sing the lay of the old empire. But again a matter of critical consequence—our increasing alignment with the United States—was not the subject of extensive popular debate. This is not to argue, retroactively, against the need for military cooperation with the United States during the war. But there is a vast difference between wartime cooperation and a North American alliance leading to permanent integration. This, unlike conscription, was not the subject of any plebiscite.

6) Canadian policy makers played an important role in the coming of the Cold War. Indeed, in their hubris, some even claimed parenthood of the North American Alliance. Why should Canadian policy makers, so conspicuous in their reserve regarding European entanglements of the 1920s and 1930s, have shifted so abruptly into high diplomatic gear after 1945? What were the stakes for them, and why were they so committed to an anti-Soviet alliance?

It seems that ideology and stragegic interests underpinned their stance. Where ideology was concerned, anti-communism was a particularly attractive variant within our counter-revolutionary culture. Having found even 18th-century liberal revolutions too much to swallow, could our political leaders have found anything agreeable in 20th-century communist ones? Not easily. Anti-communism also had the advantage of appealing to conservative Catholic sentiment in Quebec, as well as to various shades of Protestant belief in English Canada.

I am not trying to paint an attractive picture of Stalinist Russia or to downplay the nature of Soviet domination in Eastern Europe. But European imperialism—in India, Indonesia, Indo-China or Africa—and 20th-century American imperialism, had not been particularly edifying. Nor were some of the regimes we embraced in the name of the Western Alliance paragons of liberal or democratic values. Yet Canadian policy makers had no difficulties living with them.

In a way, the ideology of the Cold War allowed Canadian politicians to partake, if only vicariously, in the kind of moralistic crusade Canadians had never experienced during the evolution from colonial status. We had never executed kings or tsars or overthrown foreign masters. As a consolation prize, Canadian policy makers could now play chaplains in the great battle between good and evil that the Cold War, for both sides, had come to symbolize.

And there were strategic interests that tied Canada firmly to the United States but also, even if decreasingly, to Europe. The North Atlantic Alliance seemed like an ideal way to put the North Atlantic triangle back together and keep the United States, Britain and France in tandem. It even kept Canadians from asking too pointed questions about junior partnership to the United States in our continental relations.

Neutralism would have required a far clearer sense of our national distinctiveness. It would have required a more national form of capitalism, such as Sweden's, and a greater concern for the exercize of our own sovereignty. After sixty-five years under the British umbrella and a decade or more under the American, Canadian policy makers were much happier in their role as junior partner.

7) The question of Quebec is a persistent one in Canadian history, going back at least to the British conquest. If 1837-38 had heralded the possibility of an independent Quebec, in some form of association with an independent Upper Canada, 1867 had led to quite a different form of federation. Quebec was in a permanent minority, the major economic levers were in Ottawa, and Britain continued to dominate foreign and military policy.

I will not dwell on the various conflicts that pitted Quebec against English Canada: the hanging of Riel, the Manitoba and Ontario school questions, the conscription crises of both wars. As for Quebec's internal politics, I would mention economic domination by English Canadians and ideological domination by a reactionary Church and an ultraconservative political elite.

It was only with the urbanization of Quebec, its industrialization, and its increased opening to the modern world that the society underwent significant modernization. This became most apparent after the death of Duplessis and the start of the Quiet Revolution.

As Quebec governments sought to make up for lost time and intervene in economic and social arenas which were neglected in the past, conflict with Ottawa increased. A new Quebec nationalism emerged, ideologically quite different from the clerical-conservative versions of the previous hundred years. It envisioned greater autonomy— or even independence—for the homeland of French Canadians.

The new nationalism brought with it a significant flowering of democratic practice. Not that Quebec suddenly became a participatory democracy, but intellectual life, trade union activity, community associations, and the political system experienced a remarkable transformation. Quebec society had become pluralistic, self-questioning, and eager for experimentation; English Canada appeared remarkably parochial by comparison.

The subsequent reaction is well known. After attempting to allay this new nationalism through modest concessions and Royal Commissions on Bilingualism and Biculturalism, the federal government adopted a hard line when Trudeau came to power in 1968. Separatism and its surrogate, Quebec nationalism, would be stopped in their tracks, through fair means or foul. Police operations had been launched before October 1970, while the October Crisis provided a golden opportunity to deal with the nationalist left in Quebec a body-blow.

The rise of the Parti Quebecois and its election in 1976 threatened this strategy. Not that the PQ was particularly radical in its constitutional or economic objectives. But it was committed to a form of Quebec sovereignty and it was prepared to wage a major struggle for this. For only the second time in Canadian history a referendum would be held, this time within the confines of a single province. Pierre Elliott Trudeau had once castigated Quebec for lacking a democratic tradition. Now Quebec proved itself more respectful of the concept of popular sovereignty than anyone else—Trudeau's government included.

The referendum to give a mandate to the government of Quebec to negotiate sovereignty-association with the rest of Canada was lost; roughly 60 percent voted against it. This set the stage for the federal-provincial negotiations of 1980-81 and Trudeau's new constitution. He had always spurned the concept of a distinct Quebec nation and was now determined to write into law his version of a united Canada. Nowhere in the new Charter of Rights is there reference to the two nations that make up this country. Nor are collective, as opposed to individual rights, even mentioned.

The question of Quebec's place within Confederation has still not been solved. The Quebec government's refusal to go along with the constitutional package, and the persistence in Quebec of strong sentiment for some sort of special status, ensure there will be future agitation. The legacy of grassroots democratic organizations of the 1960s and 1970s also lives on, haunting governments in Quebec as well as in Ottawa. For this we can be grateful.

8) We might think the issue of Canadian nationalism would touch a sensitive popular nerve in English Canada. If we can believe our economic historians, many major national projects, from the building of the railways to the establishment of the CBC or the laying of the Trans-Canada Pipeline, were examples of "defensive expansionism." That is to say, they were meant to protect significant parts of the Canadian economy and culture from American encroachment.

Since World War II there have been important instances of nationalist policies. I could mention the establishment of the Canada Council in the 1950s, the symbolic nationalism of the new flag and of Expo in the 1960s, the establishment of the Foreign Investment Review Agency in the 1970s, and the National Energy Policy of the early 1980s. I could add to this the existence of a fairly mass-based constituency for nationalism in the late sixties and early seventies, with the intellectual community, students, the trade union movement and professionals lending support. So far so good, assuming that a dose of Canadian nationalism is a reasonable thing to have.

There is, however, a problem with Canadian national-ism as we have known it. The argument may appear surprising coming from a person on the left, but I think it is necessary to take dead-aim at our statist political culture. For many on the left, public enterprise and state ownership are in and of themselves virtuous things to be opposed to private capital. In general, I would tend to concur, but with one major caveat—that such enterprises be democratically managed and controlled. The problem in Canada is that there has been too little democratic practice surrounding our state enterprises.

Thus, when provincially owned hydro companies are constituted, or national carriers like the CNR or Air Canada, or cultural agencies like the CBC and Canada Council, or, more recently, Petro-Canada, we look in vain for an ingredient of popular participation. I am not even speaking about workers' control here (though I will be returning to that later). The organization of these crown corporations is as hierarchical, as secretive, and as closed to public involvement as most any in the private sector. Their Boards of Directors do not represent a cross section of the Canadian population; the big bourgeoisie and the professional classes provide almost all of their members.

The consequence is statism with a popular culture, often American in inspiration, prevailing in the society. Statism tends to foster a top-down nationalist culture, inculcating certain truths or values into a population that otherwise would not know better. Our governments, parliaments and legislatures become the organizers of our civic consciousness. National celebrations like Expo have to be staged; nationalist propaganda is transmitted across the air waves, through the newspapers, along with our social security cheques. The concept of nation is irrevocably bound up with the idea of the state.

I do not think this is either desirable or healthy. True, in Canada the state came before the nation. At the time of Confederation the colonies, especially the English Canadian ones, lacked any national sentiment. And for the next century the state, however falteringly, tried to foster it.

Today, however, it should be possible to dissociate state from nation, and to recognize that the nation must take hold in civil society. The French historian Renan who

38

spoke of the nation as a daily plebiscite in the hearts of men (and *we* would add women and children) was not wrong. The state itself is a much less appealing affair. It is a large, cumbrous, and often alien institution that constantly needs to be opened up to the ordinary citizen.

The appropriation of Canadian nationalism by the state is one more manifestation of our parliamentary, as opposed to popular, culture. It helps legitimize the domination which those who ostensibly represent us—and the powerful executive whom they bolster—exercize *over* us. Once again, we become the objects, and not the subjects, of our history.

V
The Statist Tradition

In one sense statism is the epitome of everything our parliamentary tradition represents. In another, it embodies what some consider a tradition of public as opposed to purely private enterprise, of government as the distributor of sweet-meats, rather than as a tyrant, despot or oppressor.

When one characterizes the Canadian political culture as statist, what exactly is meant? Surely not that the state consistently overrides the institutions of civil society: corporate power, big and small; churches; trade unions; the media; the myriad of associations that make up a complex society such as ours. Only a seriously jaundiced observer of the Canadian scene, probably of neo-conservative persuasion, would depict our situation in that light.

But if by statist we mean a propensity to look to governmental authority to regulate the establishment of our communication links, or the financing of our resource-extracting projects, then there is something to the label. Writers from Innis and Creighton through Grant and the neo-Marxist political economy school of recent years have underlined the role of the state in the accumulation process of a staple-based capitalism.

What is true for economic accumulation has also increasingly been true for social services since World War II. Like other western societies, Canada has greatly expanded its social security system—unemployment insurance and family allowances in the early 1940s, universal old age pensions in the 1950s, medicare, hospital insurance, the Canada Pension Plan and comprehensive welfare services since the 1960s. The welfare state was part and parcel of the solidarities which depression and the war fostered. It flourished with the post-war prosperity of the western world, with high rates of employment and expanding G.N.P.s. And despite the fiscal crisis of the state, and the onslaught of the new right in provinces like British Columbia, it is not about to be swept away.

The tradition of a strong state is, of course, historically as much a conservative premise as a Keynesian liberal or a social democratic one. George Grant is quite correct in his *Lament for a Nation* to point to the conservative parentage of some of our important public enterprises: Ontario Hydro, the CNR, the CBC. That older conservatism may have weakened; contemporary Canadian conservatism has been redefined as a version of right-wing liberal economic thought. But it helps explain, along with "defensive expansionism," a greater propensity in Canada than in the United States to use the state as an instrument of public policy.

But is statism synonymous with democracy? Leaving Canada for a moment, and looking farther afield, we might ask whether the increased role of the 20th-century state has gone hand in hand with the exercize of power from below. Have the great revolutions of the Russian or Chinese variety given workers or peasants direct control over the Marxist-Leninist vanguard parties which rule in their names? Have authoritarian counter-revolutions of the fascist variety enhanced citizen control over the central state? Has the increased power of the state, under conservative, liberal or social democratic auspices, broadened or deepened citizen input into decision making?

I do not want to seem to be invoking some mythical earlier period that, by comparison, appears to be a golden age. It was certainly not the "night-watchman state" of classical liberalism that allowed its politically and economically disenfranchised members any meaningful form of participation. Nor did state power have more popular appeal in the absolutist states of early modern times or the great Mediterranean, Near Eastern or Asiatic empires of the ancient world.

The truth is that centralized state power and political participation do not make good bedfellows. Nor, for that matter, does any form of strongly centralized power—corporate, ecclesiastical or military—promote democratic values. The history of the Roman Catholic Church, of 20th-century warfare, and of the multinational corporation should teach us that. As Robert Michels wrote at the beginning of the 20th century, whoever speaks of large-scale organization speaks of oligarchy—power exercized by the few.

Is anarchism the answer? Not if we are thinking seriously about large-scale industrial societies, or of the nation-state in a world filled with rival and competing ones. Nor if we remember that the state helps provide much that individuals, faced with the complexities and inequalities stemming from the division of labour and the division of capital, cannot provide for themselves.

But statism by itself is an unacceptable arrangement. At its extreme, as in totalitarianisms of the Nazi or Stalinist variety, it threatens to devour the very identity of the citizen. It reduces the autonomy of civil institutions to naught. In its more familiar western guise—the corporatist-type integration of labour, capital and other social actors under the auspices of the representative state—its day-to-day operations remain removed from the lives and concerns of the ordinary citizen. Elections every four or five years do little to give that citizen the feeling that popular sovereignty is in command. The economic concentration of monopoly capitalism reinforces a sense of powerlessness.

In Canada the state is a source of strength and weakness. Statism has tied together disparate regions within a continent-wide framework, and promoted economic and social development which otherwise might never have occurred. Public enterprises have shown themselves to be a viable and successful alternative to the private corporation. A state-promoted collectivism has been the alternative to that often selfish individualism which North American capitalism so effortlessly engenders.

Yet simultaneously, the state wears the mask of authority. This, of course, was implicit in the assumptions underlying crown rights and parliamentary powers. The claim to sovereignty is potentially authoritarian, whether exercized by kings, by legislatures or by political parties. It is a claim to be imposed, by force if necessary, against all would-be dissenters in society.

The state that hovers over us is also the state that polices us. The Cabinets that grant favours also set authoritative rules to which we are expected to conform. A conservative state sets a conservative agenda, a Marxist-Leninist state a Marxist-Leninist one; the necessity to obey is no less imperative in each.

Canadian statism has inculcated into the population a tradition of deference and obedience. We expect governments to direct our behaviour, rather than the other way around. We see Parliaments and legislatures as incarnating the majesty of state, and forget that only popular impulse gives them life and breath. By elevating governments over us, we elevate them into a power against us, and give them the weapons with which to make us bow

43

low. Statism is the distorted lens through which sovereignty of the people becomes sovereignty over the people.

It is ironic that in Canada today the strongest oppostion to the state comes from the right, rather than the left. There is a profound misunderstanding involved. Historically the right is a much firmer believer in the virtues of obedience and deference than is the left. Moreover, it can be argued that the Canadian state has enhanced the operation of capitalism rather than undercut it. How ungrateful of our latter-day Friedmanites to bite the hand of the institution that, more than any other, has allowed capitalist relations of production to flourish.

But it is equally striking to see with what enthusiasm the left has identified itself with a statist tradition that betrays a strongly anti-democratic flavour. The same governments which created crown corporations suppressed strikes and popular movements without flinching. The state which introduced social or labour legislation could—through the tax system, bounties or subsidies—shower far greater concessions on all the nabobs of the land. The sovereignty of which parliaments spoke was one which governments have ensured would not rest in *our* hands.

When one thinks further of the extremes state power has been taken to by various regimes of the left, the need for a serious reappraisal appears imperative. It will not do for members of the left in Canada to wrap themselves in the mantle of statism as the major alternative to corporate power. Nothing could be less likely to win popular support and more certain to play into the hands of those who consider socialism and totalitarianism to be one and the same thing. If we think back to the genesis of socialism, even to some of the writings of Marx and Engels, socialism had a profoundly anti-statist dimension. It looked to self-governing producers and communities of workers as an alternative to the centralized state. It was the left, not

44

the right, who talked about the withering away of the state, about maximizing democracy and popular sovereignty, about eliminating the bureaucratic and military apparati of the bourgeoisie.

It is no accident that many on the European left in the 1980s are increasingly disenchanted with purely statist solutions and want to develop democratic alternatives. Just as the overly centralized state moves us unwittingly toward nuclear annihilation, undiluted state ownership connotes an absence of citizen and working class control in other spheres. The same impulse which underlies the peace movement also motivates concerns about workplace democracy, environmental protection and decentralized economic and political decision making. Left-wing political culture must be transformed in the industrialized countries. The West German Green Party represents one important move in this direction; there are similar tendencies at work elsewhere.

This suggests that the Canadian left needs to carry its analysis well beyond the statism of the CCF-NDP or, *a fortiori*, of the Communist Party of Canada. It suggests that the amalgam of nationalism and the state, which the Waffle Movement spoke for in the 1960s and which the recent Laxer Report has reiterated, is entirely inadequate as an ideological response to the times. The left will do better to rethink the political structures around which it hopes to build its New Jerusalem, to put democracy and decentralization at the very top of its agenda. A critique of parliamentarism in the name of a participatory political culture constitutes part of the potential break with statism. The search for alternative economic arrangements can move us beyond the old formula: socialism = state ownership. It is to a remaking of left culture, no less than of Canadian political culture, that this essay invites the reader.

VI
Constitutional Bonapartism

Our constitution—the 1980-82 package that is—was presented to the Canadian public as the final stage in our emancipation from Britain. Fifty years after the Statute of Westminster, following repeated and fruitless attempts to work out agreement with the provinces, Canada was at last to gain the powers of constitutional amendment commensurate "with the status of an independent state." Acts of the United Kingdom Parliament would no longer apply to this country—115 years after Confederation!

For good measure, we got a Charter of Rights and Freedoms which had been sorely lacking in the original B.N.A. Act. Civil libertarians and others had long pointed to the inadequate protection for individual rights under our parliamentary system; any act of Parliament or a legislature could obliterate existing rights. There had been instances enough, especially during wars and political crises such as October 1970, when real abuses had occurred.

Theoretically, this twin package of rights and a Canadian amendment formula should have signalled a new dawn. It suggested a maturing of Canadian democracy and an end to whatever lingering colonialism might have surrounded our earlier development. Surely what had or hadn't happened in 1867 now made no difference. Nor did it matter whether we had had a counter-revolutionary tradition or whether some of our 20th-century experiences were less than uplifting. Trudeau and nine of the Premiers had wiped the slate clean overnight. The true north strong and free glistened in the cold, but radiant, sun.

A good number of Canadians were naive enough to believe this account, to accept as manna from heaven the "gifts" which Trudeau and his negotiating partners bestowed. Oh, there had been controversy about the procedures used by the "feds"—eight of the provinces had originally balked. There had been criticisms of the original charter from civil libertarians, women's groups, and native people; but these too had been largely allayed. Except for some predictable grumbling from separatists in Quebec, all seemed well. Even our three federal parties were united, in a rare instance that suggested Canadian consensus at its best.

But a fairy tale it was and will remain. Like the daughters of Pelias seduced by Medea into believing they could make their father young again, Canadians were beguiled into believing they had discovered the secret of eternal youth. Our constitutional debates, however, did not produce a rejuvenated body politic.

Let me state, with no equivocation, my abhorrence for the constitutional charade we were subjected to. My catalogue of grievances includes the Bonapartist procedures used by the federal government, the reinforcement of parliamentary sovereignty which followed, the complicity of the premiers, the irrelevance of the appeals to the Supreme Court, and the indignity that the whole affair has inflicted on democratic practice in this country. I would also want to address the gaping defects of the so-called "Charter of Rights"—but without getting lost in legalistic

47

arguments. There has been all too much law and not enough politics in our discussions of this Canada Act already.

When I accuse Pierre Elliott Trudeau of Bonapartism I am, of course, not using the term literally—there was no "whiff of grapeshot" as in 1795, no overthrowing of an elected assembly as in 1851. Bonapartism, however, has larger connotations: 1) it evokes a leader's ambition—one which approaches megalomania—to leave his permanent mark on the history and institutions of a country; 2) it suggests a claim to legitimacy for his actions that overrides existing conventions and procedures; 3) it suggests heavy-handed domination by the executive arm of the state.

Trudeau's ambition to go down in Canadian history as the man who patriated the constitution was not, in itself, objectionable. Canada should never have permitted Britain to retain powers over it in the first place. Nor would I criticize his desire to see a bill of rights inscribed in the Canadian constitution, however inadequate I find the Charter of Rights we ended up with.

But megalomania enters on two scores. First, the desire to entrench his own version of liberal philosophy as the official one for all time to come was a serious misuse of power. All the freedoms the bill speaks of are individual ones: legal rights, equality rights, language rights and so on. It seems to have escaped our Lycurgus that in our century some of the most important rights pertain to groups rather than individuals. This was no accidental omission; it reflects Trudeau's philosophy going back to his acerbic essays of the late 1950s and early 1960s, which denounce Quebec nationalism and other forms of collectivism.

But is it so clear that language rights pertain to individuals rather than to national or sub-national groupings? Is it really so outlandish in the late 20th century

48

to suggest that workers have certain rights, e.g. to organize, or that citizens have certain economic rights, e.g. to employment and reasonable living standards? Do these "national" rights or "class" rights or "social" rights not belong in a modern-day charter? Yet they were omitted only because they did not jive with Trudeau's Actonian view of the world. By denying their existence, he no doubt hoped that they would go away.

If Trudeau sought to arrest history where rights were concerned, this was even more patent regarding Quebec. The section on official languages and minority language educational rights takes up a good one-third of the Charter. This is extraordinary, considering how much less important these are than the fundamental freedoms *sketchily* outlined in the short paragraph of clause two. Quite clearly a political intention was at work: to entrench official bilingualism and minority language rights as a permanent bulwark against the sirens of Quebec separatism.

An important element of deceit entered here. On May 20, 1980, the night of the Quebec referendum, Trudeau suggested that he had understood the aspirations of Quebecers—those who had voted yes or no—for constitutional change. The *status quo* would no longer suffice. His words seemed to imply that some form of special status—intermediary between sovereignty-associ-ation and existing federalism—might finally be in the cards.

Trudeau, it turned out, had stolen a leaf from his old enemy, de Gaulle. The General, visiting Algiers in the early 1960s, told the partisans of "L'Algerie francaise" who had put him into power in 1958: "Je vous ai compris." Within a year he signed the Evian Accords, giving Algeria independence. Trudeau had similarly understood nothing, save his desire to write his own version of federalism into tablets of stone. No wonder Claude Ryan and many

Quebec provincial Liberals felt betrayed by Trudeau's fall offensive. Like all the Bonapartes of this world, Trudeau placed his glory ahead of sibylline promises to a divided Quebec.

Existing conventions and procedures were now swept aside to rush the constitution into place. Trudeau was prepared to offer the provinces a take-it-or-leave-it package, and when eight of them rejected it, go over their heads directly to Westminster. The irony of using the old imperial authority one last time to ram through fundamental constitutional reforms is too delicious to overlook.

In the end this did not quite work; there were the parliamentary amendments to the text, the effective lobby mounted by the provinces in London (another bit of irony), and the decision of our own Supreme Court on constitutional proprieties. Nonetheless, if we compare the final package with the original federal version, we are struck by how much Trudeau did get his own way.

This illustrates the great power which has become concentrated in the person, as much as in the office, of Prime Minister. Trudeau dominated his federal caucus. Had they not begged him to resume leadership when, playing Cincinnatus, he had momentarily resigned during the brief bout of opposition in 1979? He dominated both houses of Parliament, our antediluvian Senate with its permanent Liberal majority, no less than the Commons. And he exercized increasing power vis-a-vis the provinces, both through Ottawa's enhanced economic and fiscal clout which followed several decades of retreat and through his personal role in helping to secure a "No" result in the Quebec referendum. Constitutional Bonapartism defines his role perfectly.

But let's not let this metaphor run away with the discussion. Sovereignty in this country had been grounded in Parliament for over a century. The new constitution was calculated to reinforce this. Was it not Parliament which debated the original resolution and then embarked upon extensive televised committee hearings? Was Trudeau's entire constitutional strategy not based on the presumption that it was the exclusive right of the Canadian Parliament to send constitutional resolutions to Westminster? Did Parliament not retain a lion's share of the power over future constitutional amendments? And, more tellingly still, was parliamentarism not defined as the very essence of democracy in the text of this new Charter?

Clauses three to five of the Charter are headed by the title "Democratic Rights." It is worth reproducing this short section in its entirety.

Democratic Rights

3. Democratic rights of citizens.

Every citizen of Canada has the right to vote in an election of members of the House of Commons or of a legislative assembly and to be qualified for membership therein.

4. Maximum duration of legislative bodies.

(1) No House of Commons and no legislative assembly shall continue for longer than five years from the date fixed for the return of the writs at a general election of its members.

(2) In time of real or apprehended war, invasion or insurrection, a House of Commons may be continued by Parliament and a legislative assembly may be continued by the legislature beyond five years if such continuation is not opposed by the votes of more than one-third of the members of the House of Commons or the legislative assembly, as the case may be.

5. Annual sitting of the legislative bodies.
There shall be a sitting of Parliament and of each legislature at least once every twelve months.

What we have here is the attempt, for the first time since the "peace, order and good government" clause of 1867, to state the philosophy of the Canadian political system. The word "democracy" is now in greater vogue so it will be harnessed to the task. And what does democracy amount to, according to our new Fathers of Confederation? Very simply, to the right of citizens to vote for members of the House of Commons and provincial legislatures and to be eligible themselves for election to these bodies. The remainder of our "Democratic Rights," in language reminiscent of the British Bill of Rights of 1689, are reduced to the requirement for annual sittings of Parliament and for its periodic renewal.

Some may say that surely, this is what democracy is all about. And if they were to confine themselves to some of the mainstream liberal writings on democracy over the last fifty years, they would probably be right. It was Joseph Schumpeter, in his *Capitalism, Socialism and Democracy* of 1942, who reduced democracy to an electoral choice between competing sets of candidates. Robert Dahl, Giovanni Sartori and other writers have since echoed this argument.

Is voting in parliamentary elections, however, the sum total of democratic theory? Does political participation begin and end with the ballot box? Does the ordinary citizen go into political hibernation during the four-or five-year intervals between legislative elections? This is what the text of our Charter suggests, and what its presumable author, Pierre Elliott Trudeau, has on occasion implied.

Here is the quintessential statement, not of democracy, but of its parliamentary stepsister. If rule by the people is the etymological meaning of democracy, how far we have strayed! From the direct democracy of ancient Athens, or the popular aspirations of all the great revolutions— English, American, French or Russian—to this narrow encapsulation of democratic theory. The people have but one political function: to choose their legislators. These legislators retain all the rights and powers arrogated by 19th-century parliamentarians but with a new twist: they can now confound democracy with sovereignty of Parliament. The word "democracy" should be struck from our Charter, and clauses three to five retitled "Voting Rights" or better still, "The Rights of Parliament."

Back in 1646-48, Leveller tracts spoke of "An Agreement of the People" as something which came not from Parliament, but from the people themselves. Have we made so little progress that it now appears heretical to suggest that Parliament was not the legitimate body to draft our Constitution? That only the people can give the mandate to devise a constitution, and that neither Trudeau nor Parliament nor the Premiers nor the legislatures had any such mandate?

We have come back full circle to the theme of popular vs. parliamentary sovereignty. In a system of the first kind, major constitutional change would require some elected Constituent Assembly or Convention, distinct from a sitting Parliament or legislature, with an express mandate to redraft the fundamental laws by which we are governed. This law would be above Parliament and therefore not for Parliament itself to enunciate. The text would have to be submitted to the population for approval. Only after its ratification by a clear majority in a referendum, preferably in all of the major regions, could it become law. All subsequent amendments would require similar approval.

This sounds like a tall order, and maybe it is. But

53

popular democracy is a more cumbersome affair than parliamentary liberalism. Democracy requires greater participation by the citizenry than parliamentary government is prepared to cede. It is a formidable challenger to parliamentary monopolies, and a continuous reminder that all are capable of directly participating in the business of governing. Popular democracy is the unhappy consciousness of the parliamentary system.

No wonder the word "people" was so studiously omitted from the text of the Charter. Instead, the opening passage speaks of "the supremacy of God and the rule of law." Did our bold parliamentarians believe we were living in the 17th century or perchance, the 14th? Did they take us for fools, duped by their self-serving game?

I will have more to say about popular democracy shortly. For the moment, it is enough to underline just how much the old tradition of parliamentary sovereignty carried over into the constitutional revisions of 1980-82. *Plus ca change, plus c'est la meme chose.*

Let me add a little about the role of the Premiers and the courts. The Premiers had no better claim to speak for their electorates on constitutional questions than the federal government did. Not one of them had been given an explicit mandate to negotiate a charter of rights, amendment formula or anything else, and they can be rightly accused of *lese-souverainete*. Provincial governments have significant powers under our federal system, and it is perfectly reasonable that they make their views known on the federal-provincial distribution of powers and such matters. But in the last resort, their claims to engage in constitution making rested on the same false doctrine of parliamentary sovereignty as the federal government's They were substituting their own wills for the will of the people.

What we saw between 1980-82, therefore, was a modern-day version of the old boy's club of the

Confederation Debates. Trudeau and the Premiers, with all their ministers and advisers, negotiated over our heads about the fundamental principles by which the political system was to be conducted. There was a conflict of interest involved, which they conveniently overlooked. How could those charged with the *day-to-day* business of governing also be trusted to come up with the *long-term* rules to which they and their successors would be bound? Were these men (there were precious few women) our elected representatives, or self-appointed constitution makers? Does the first function in any way imply the second?

When we pose these questions, we begin to realize just how shaky the scaffolding of the Canada Act really is. Federal-provincial conferences by government leaders had no real constitutional status. The months of posturing, back and forth, between Ottawa and the provinces made good melodrama but bad democratic politics. The final ignominious round of negotiations in Ottawa hotel rooms in November 1981 stamped "Approved" on what had been, from the start, an illegitimate procedure.

Nor did the various judicial appeals improve matters. It was all very nice to give Supreme Court judges a new feeling of self-importance. Had their American counterparts not enjoyed the same since Chief Justice Marshall's power grab of the early 19th century? But the writing of a constitution, as opposed to its interpretation, is not something we need to involve the judiciary in. Were our Supreme Court judges such Solomons that we should fall on bended knee before their judgements? Could *they* be trusted to provide what was so sadly deficient in the process from the beginning—popular participation? Not very likely. Indeed, the Supreme Court judgement merely reinforced the public's impression that constitutional debate is the reserve domain of politicians and lawyers.

In the constitutional hijacking that took place, the loser

was democracy. Trudeau may have emerged with enhanced prestige; history will determine that. The federal government and the provinces may have horse traded with each other. Parliament and the Supreme Court may have extracted shreds of glory from the inglorious affair. The people(s) of Canada in their collective capacity were not such winners. Held to a passive role through most of the deliberations, they were expected to remain passive under the new constitution. Lawyers might engage in endless litigation over the individual rights contained in the Charter, but sovereignty remains with our political elites. The people sit on mutely in the stalls.

VII
A Constituent Assembly

Popular democracy would have entailed a different sequence of events from what went on in our recent constitutional gambit. The resulting package would have been dramatically different from what we ended up with. Let me examine these two propositions a little more closely.

If our traditions had been less steeped in parliamentarism, less counter-revolutionary, and more democratically inclined, what might have happened? For a start, the proposal for constitutional reform would not have come exclusively from above. Among the two major linguistic communities there would have been a widely held desire for constitutional change. Citizen's groups would have formed, political parties would have been mobilized, and a full-fledged debate might have embraced large sections of society. Constitution making in a democracy should be an educational affair and should entail extensive political participation. After all, a society is attempting to pronounce itself not on some passing political programme, but on the fundamentals by which it is to be bound.

Canadians have never been through such an exercize. The sham of the 1860s was as undemocratic an affair as one could find. And the people's role in subsequent constitutional amendments was no greater. Canadians, as a result, have always found their constitutional history boring. But then no one has ever asked them to come up with something better.

Let us imagine, miracle of miracles, that this had occurred in 1980. That after a decade or more of federal-provincial bickering, after two decades of Quebec nationalism and a renewal of Canadian nationalism, the decision had been made to rethink the foundations of this country. *Nota bene*, I did not say to patriate the B.N.A. Act. That document had been unsatisfactory back in 1867, and no patriation was going to make it more viable in the 1980s. The monarchy was irrelevant to Canada, the appointed Senate was a scandal, and even the federal-provincial distribution of powers needed a major rethinking. As to what the B.N.A. Act did not contain—a bill of rights, an acknowledgement of our binational character, an extended discussion of the functions of government in the modern world, an assertion of popular democracy—the less said the better. The shrewdest move would have been to have allowed this act to moulder untouched in London and to begin afresh.

How should we have proceeded? I suggested earlier that an elected Constituent Assembly would have been the appropriate body to undertake this task. By this I mean an assembly distinct from both Parliament and the legislatures, elected by the population as a whole with the specific mandate to devise an entirely new constitution.

Such an assembly, to avoid any conflict of interests, should have had members who were not simultaneously sitting in any other elected body. In other words, MPs and MLAs, whether Prime Ministers, Cabinet Ministers, or ordinary members, could not have taken a seat in this Assembly without first resigning from any other that they held. Election to this Assembly should not have been along federal constituency lines; some variant of proportional representation on a provincial or even regional level would have made more sense. The membership of such a body, to function effectively, should not have exceeded 150, about half the size of our actual Commons. Special measures could have been taken to ensure that native peoples were represented and, if we really wanted to be radical (and ensure a lot of new faces), we might have provided for a 50-50 division between men and women in its ranks.

I imagine the majority of those elected would have been chosen on the basis of some party affiliation. But it is likely that individuals of particular distinction would also have been elected to this body. The electoral campaign which preceded the Assembly's establishment would have provided an opportunity for far-ranging discussion of all the issues that a modern constitution encompasses. It would have fostered grassroots politicization around certain core questions, in a way that the 1980-82 procedure largely prevented.

If we imagine such an Assembly had been constituted, what might it have looked like? It would certainly have been anything but monolithic. Advocates of Quebec independence would have sat next to committed federalists, defenders of provincial powers beside committed centralizers, monarchists beside republicans, socialists beside stalwarts of the right. At first glance this sounds not like a formula for constitution making, but for disaster.

Sociologically, however, this Assembly would have reflected the constitutional views of Canadians a lot more effectively than either the federal Parliament or the legislatures. What is more, having a direct mandate from the entire country would have given it the legitimacy to proceed, unbeholden to either level of government. That mandate would also have entailed a heightened responsibility to succeed, however long it took to thrash out the more difficult questions. It would also have required

59

ongoing participation of all sectors of opinion, as different aspects of the constitution came up for discussion.

We are obviously in no position to prejudge the details of the document which might have resulted. It would, however, have had to address issues that our actual constitution makers avoided. It would have had to contain alternatives to some of the structures we presently have.

For example, it is inconceivable to me that such an Assembly would not have opted for an element of popular sovereignty. This would have been strongly reinforced by the need to win majority electoral approval for any draft. The language of this document would therefore have been significantly closer to that of constitutions written under the impulse of popular mobilization. Not that the spirit of revolution, liberal or other, would have presided over our Constituent Assembly's deliberations. But neither would the ghosts of parliaments past have triumphed so effortlessly.

Such an Assembly would have had to face the national realities of Canada. If sovereignty-association were no longer on the agenda after the Quebec referendum, some recognition of Quebec's unique character remained imperative. The Pepin-Robarts Report had moved timidly in this direction—a Constituent Assembly would have had to face it head-on. Would Quebec have been granted powers not given to other provinces, such as over social security or culture? Would this have entailed a right to opt out of certain federal programmes or a formal transfer of powers? If this proved too radical, perhaps statements recognizing Quebec's unique character as the homeland of French Canadians would have done the trick. Either way, we would have moved some distance beyond the homilies of the Official Languages Act and toward a franker recognition of the dualistic character of the country.

The question of native rights would also have had to be tackled. For a start, an Assembly might have repudiated

60

some of the unequal treaties imposed on native peoples in the past and accepted the need for major compensation for expropriated lands. It might have recognized that native peoples had the right to autonomous political administration (dare I suggest self-determination?) in the areas they control, and just possibly, the right to provincial status in the north.

Several of our political institutions would have come in for discussion or reform. The monarchy, a sacrosanct institution for some, would have at least been the subject of extensive debate. Public opinion in Quebec has for decades been hostile to this institution which is a vestige of the British imperial past. In English Canada, republican feeling has also been growing of late, though it has lacked a focus. In the debates of the Constituent Assembly, this issue would have come into the open. Those who wished to preserve the British monarchy as the symbol of the *Canadian* state, and this in the late 20th century, would have been forced to scramble for arguments. They would have had to justify the maintenance of this particular symbol, when all our other constitutional links with Britain were finally being severed. They would have had to explain why a hereditary *foreign* monarch would be more appropriate than an appointed or elected Canadian President. The pyrotechnics around this one issue would have brought the whole constitutional exercize alive. We can imagine the Royal Canadian Legion and the Daughters of the Empire out one day, and a nascent Republican League the next. Why, this business of the constitution could have become rejuvenating!

The Senate is a good deal less likely to have survived intact. If this institution is meant to reflect the federal nature of the country, it is wholly inadequate to the task. There were two routes we could have gone to achieve this end. The first is a variant of the American or Australian system of directly elected senators who represent states

61

rather than smaller constituencies. The second is a House of the Provinces a la the West German Bundesrat, with provincial governments (or better yet, the legislatures) selecting the delegations. There is no need to go into the details—we would have ended up with a different second house.

I doubt a Constituent Assembly would have been seriously interested in restructuring the House of Commons. But it would have had to make up for the B.N.A. Act's silence regarding the executive branch of government. There is no reference in the B.N.A. Act to either the Prime Minister or the Cabinet, despite the enormous powers of each. Nor is there any mention of the civil service, or of crown corporations. A modern-day constitution would have had to outline their powers and responsibilities, their relationship to the legislative branch of government, and more importantly still, their responsibility to the people. An updated discussion of the judicial function could also have been expected.

A hoarier problem to resolve would have been the federal-provincial distribution of powers. Given the way a Constituent Assembly would have been elected, it is unlikely that extreme provincialist or federalist positions could have prevailed. But the provinces might have fared a good deal better in the enumeration of their powers than in 1867. This would simply have meant adjusting constitutional language to 20th-century realities. There might have been some trade-off of particular responsibilities between the federal and provincial levels. The federal government would, nonetheless, have preserved major responsibility for the economy and for a good deal of social policy. In international affairs, federal primacy would have been underlined, but the provinces' role in matters which came under their jurisdiction would have been clarified. There would probably have been mention of some of Canada's international commitments, e.g. to the United Nations, the

Commonwealth or la Francophonie.

How might the Constituent Assembly have addressed the issue of rights? A large majority would likely have favoured a codified bill of rights. The real question would have been what kind. Most of the individual rights outlined in our present Charter would have been included, though one hopes in more inspiring language. The absurd opting-out provisions for Parliament and legislatures in clause 33 of our present Charter would not have been there.

I suspect there would have been a move to enlarge the definition of rights to include social and economic ones. Such rights are part and parcel of most West European constitutions and there is no good reason for their omission from ours. The language provisions of our present Charter, on the other hand, would have been significantly toned down, with symbolic recognition perhaps being given to the existence of national, as well as individual, rights. As for property rights, they might well have been inserted into the text, but with clear recognition of the existence of a public. and not only a private, dimension, to property.

Quebec might or might not have retained a veto power over constitutional amendments. Much more likely would have been provision for referenda on future amendments. A Constituent Assembly would have had less reason to fear this procedure than the Prime Minister and the Premiers.

These speculations about a putative Constituent Assembly are all in the realm of the possible. I have not assumed a sudden radicalization of public opinion, nor a state which is anything but an advanced capitalist one of the western variety. A Constituent Assembly could easily have undertaken much of what I have sketched here. It would have constituted a more exhilarating and rewarding experience for all Canadians than the process which we were put through.

The resulting package, for all its inevitable compromises, would have had greater appeal in all regions of the country than the Canada Act has. It would have been the result of widespread discussions and democratic elections that no one could challenge. Neither the West nor Quebec would have had reason to fear that Trudeau or any one else was pulling a fast one. Provincial powers might have been increased in some areas, but federal in others. Quebec might finally have achieved symbolic recognition as a nation, but Canadian federalism would have remained intact. The powers and responsibilities of the various branches of government would have been spelled out clearly, and the rights of Canadians even more so, in a Charter of Rights. We would have written ourselves an entirely new constitution, and proclaimed it by ourselves following its ratification by the Canadian people. We would have been several steps ahead in national sovereignty as well as in democratic practice.

Of course, things might not have gone so smoothly. Perhaps the Assembly would have dead-locked on an issue. Or some major region might have balked at the package, casting doubt on its popular legitimacy. Or the British might have decided enough was enough and sent us back the B.N.A. Act, whether we wanted it or not.

Common sense would likely have prevailed in the end; among those elected to the Assembly the impetus to reach agreement would have been strong enough to overcome most differences. It certainly would have been worthwhile to have attempted. It would have been enormously educational for the entire country. And it might have given a genuinely popular touch to our political culture. Is it any wonder that our elected legislators—federal and provincial—decided otherwise?

VIII
Participatory Democratic Theory

Parliamentary democracy as we know it in Canada falls far short of an ideal model of popular government. If anything, it militates strongly against most forms of citizen participation in political affairs. The lessons of our constitutional fiasco are fairly straightforward. We must discover ways of extending democracy into our daily lives and of rethinking the relationship between citizen and state—federal, provincial and local. We also have to re-examine the compatibility between a capitalist framework and a democratic society and see if we cannot come up with a more egalitarian arrangement.

Fortunately, in setting out in search of alternative models we are not forced to begin from zero. Not that there are ready-made models of participatory democracy out there waiting to be adapted to Canada; such models, at least at the national level, are few and far between. Even where versions exist, as in Yugoslavia, the difficulties of political cross-fertilization make it unlikely they could be adapted to Canada without major adjustments. In any case, we would need to develop our own model. We have been paying a high enough price as it is for living with branch-plant institutions in our politics and economy.

65

When I speak of models of participatory democracy, I am referring as much to a theoretical literature as to any specific examples. There is a venerable tradition attached to the concept of participation which goes all the way back to the Greeks. It is this which I would like to invoke in searching for alternatives to a purely representative system.

One crucial difference between direct democracy of the Athenian kind (or of the kind which Rousseau and occasionally Jefferson hankered after) and what we have today comes down to a question of capacities. To what degree do we think the average citizen is in fact capable of exercizing his or her judgement on major political issues? For the defenders of representative government, this is an open-and-shut question. In their view the average citizen is not particularly sensitized to the problems of the day, nor does he or she have any particular desire to be consulted on such matters. The great strength of a representative system, they argue, is that it allows the delegation of power to men (and much less frequently to women) who, while not always wise, are nonetheless able to exercize judgement for their fellow citizens. The rest of us are free to get on with our daily lives, unburdened by impossible demands from the political sphere.

This is reminiscent of the parable which Dostoyevsky recounts in the "Grand Inquisitor" passage of *The Brothers Karamazov*: Christ has returned to earth, to Seville, in the midst of the burning fires of the Inquisition. The Grand Inquisitor has Christ arrested and, in a famous dialogue, excoriates him for seeking to undo the work of the earthly Church. Christ, the Inquistor argues, has tried to teach mankind an impossible thing—freedom. But men want bread (and he could add, for North American ears, stereos and sports cars and jacuzzis) more than they want freedom. The Church will worry about the metaphysical problems, while ordinary citizens get on with the ordinary

66

problems of existence. Freedom, the Inquisitor suggests, does not rank high among these.

Defenders of representative government may find the comparison scandalous. Surely, they might retort, the right to vote in free elections is not trivial, nor were they for one moment making light of the individual freedoms, such as the freedoms of speech or of conscience, with which the Grand Inquisitor would dispense. True, political participation may not be a supreme value in their lexicon. But are they to be blamed if the ordinary citizen seems content to follow other gods?

Perhaps another parable will help. This one goes back to one of the earlier Socratic dialogues, where Plato opposes the figure of his still-young master to one of the older Sophists of Periclean Athens, Protagoras. Socrates argues that political capacity is an art which must be mastered, much like the piloting of a ship, or the healing of the body. Not all have equal capacities to engage in such occupations. If anything, politics requires even greater abilities than the other two. (In a later work of Plato's, the *Politicus*, Socrates calls politics the kingly art.)

Protagoras rejects Socrates' arguments. In rebuttal, he invokes a legend of the creation of the world, when the gods were distributing gifts to mankind. To some went beauty, to others stealth, to others physical strength, and so on. But when the question of political capacity arose, Zeus refused to make any such allocation. Since all must live in political society, all would share in the skills necessary for its governance. There is an implied equality, *isonomia*, where political capacity is concerned.

Defenders of representative government may not be impressed. Nor, we can be certain, was Plato. But does not Protagoras's ideal, in fact, correspond to the democratic ethos? There may not be complete equality of political capacity in modern societies. Some are, indeed, better informed than others. Some have superior verbal or communicative skills. Fundamentally, however, defenders of participatory democracy subscribe to the notion that the ordinary citizen is capable of exercizing a judgement on political matters which is no less valid than the judgements of the wise or the wealthy. We adhere to Protagoras's creation myth that political skill is not beyond the ken of the ordinary citizen. The question then becomes, "Why is this capacity not better mobilized?"

We here encounter a second problem with participation, that of scale. Athens in the 5th and 4th centuries B.C. was a city-state of 200,000-300,000 inhabitants. Slaves, women and foreigners had no political rights. The actual number of adult male citizens could not have greatly exceeded 50,000. Not all of these attended each meeting of the *ecclesia* or assembly. Moreover, executive authority was delegated to a council, whose 500 members were elected by lot from among the ten tribes. The assembly usually met several times a month and retained the ultimate political authority.

What relevance, critics would argue, could this have for the politics of the nation-state? Surely 20 or 50 or 200 million citizens cannot be expected to conduct their affairs on the basis of direct democracy. Rousseau might have dreamed of reviving this model in his idealized reading of the Swiss agrarian cantons; Jefferson may have regretted that the American constitution did not provide for ward democracy, side by side with the federal government, the states and the counties; but is the Athenian model not defective in the first place, and inapplicable to the modern world?

The case for participation, however, does not hinge on the Athenian model alone. Nor are we altogether helpless in the face of the larger numbers in the contemporary state. What we have to do is determine whether an element of direct participation is possible under the conditions prevailing in a country such as Canada.

Quite obviously, a direct democracy that rests upon slavery or the exploitation of women can be no model for us. Nor am I suggesting that we pack it in as a continent-wide state and go back a couple of stages in history to a city-state system. That might do as political fiction, not as political theory.

A clue to overcoming our predicament may lie with our 18th-century thinkers. Rousseau, in his writings on Poland, a large nation-state in terrible need of reform (Has anything changed?), did not indulge in his fantasy about elders deliberating underneath an oak. He suggested that, at best, Poland could be broken down into smaller units, each of which might allow for some citizen democracy. A representative system of government would continue to function at the national level. This is rather vague— Rousseau was not a very precise thinker. (Not really a political *scientist*, I can hear some of my erstwhile colleagues snorting over their drinks!) Rousseau's imprecision, for all that, may be more fruitful here than all the electoral studies of Canadian politics lined back to back.

What Rousseau was hinting at, and Jefferson as well in his passing references to ward democracy, was the need for at least one level of government where citizens could participate directly. This would obviously have to be small enough to allow for the kind of person-to-person contact that characterized the assemblies in Athens. It could not, however, supplant the representative structures which were the inevitable by-product of the nation-state.

If we examine some of the 20th-century arguments in favour of participatory democracy, we encounter similar ideas. Some writers, like C.B. Macpherson, invoke pyramidal forms of authority, without calling for the complete elimination of representative institutions. Others, like Jane Mansbridge, document instances of direct democracy in New England small-town meetings or in the work place. She does not assume that direct democracy eliminates the need for delegated political authority. Even in those few countries which have attempted to introduce features of direct democracy—Yugoslavia with workers' councils, Algeria with agricultural co-ops during the Ben Bella period, Chile under Allende—there has not been a return to the city-state or an eclipse of centralized authority.

Scale, then, need not be the overriding problem. Rather, we must try to find a way of combining direct democracy with the representative form of politics we have today. How do we re-create direct person-to-person politics in a large-scale and dispersed society? Can we do this without throwing all existing political institutions overboard? Is there some level of authority that has eluded us until now and which might be the missing link?

The level, I think, is Jefferson's level, or what I prefer to call the base-unit level. It must be small enough for citizens to gather, to deliberate and to discuss. We want to be sure than they are not limited to strictly neighbourhood concerns, but can also address the larger issues of the day. We want these base units to feed into the larger political system, so that they exercize real influence on the representative structures and can themselves initiate change. To make our political system more participatory, we must, therefore, envisage fundamental changes.

Before I elaborate some ideas about base-level democracy, let us consider another aspect of participation. We have talked about political capacities and about size and scale. How do we deal with economic distribution and with control over the goods and resources of a society?

I raise this question here, not because I want to get drawn into a lengthy debate about socialism vs. capitalism. This is a huge topic, which obviously colours any 20th-century definition of democracy, including my own. I raise it because the idea of equality was fundamental to the original Greek conception of democracy. To its enemies,

70

democracy was the regime of the equalizers, of those who would drag the rich down to the same level as the poor. For writers like Aristotle, democracy was synonymous with the rule of the poor.

In practice things were never so simple. Athens, at the time of the Peloponnesian War and after, had its own class structure with divisions between rich and poor. And nothing in the 2500 years since Pericles' time suggests that a truly classless society looms on the immediate horizon. Contemporary disillusionment with the Soviet experience and the evolution of Chinese society since Mao's death should teach us that.

But how much inequality can we accept and still claim to be democratic? A five to one ratio between the poor and the rich? A ten to one? A 30 to one as in most western societies today? A 50 to one or 100 to one, as in many countries of the third world?

Economic participation, moreover, has little meaning as long as a small number of directors or stockholders have control over huge assets, employ thousands upon thousands of people, and are free to re-invest their profits wherever or however they choose. While there may be a good case for allowing the small entrepreneur—the farmer or the little businessman—to flourish, can the case be made for the large corporation or financial institution?

Liberal theorists and neo-conservatives will, of course, defend the unbridled marketplace as the best of all possible worlds. But there are more worlds than these Horatios have ever dreamed of in their economics. We could, for example, decide that corporate power is too dangerous and nationalize every enterprise over a certain size. The danger is that we might then find ourselves face-to-face with an all powerful state, the other facet of the Minotaur in our century. And it is certainly not obvious that this would bring us any closer to a participatory type of economy.

Or we could seek to regulate the large corporation more

71

stringently, catapulting public-interest defenders onto their boards of directors, or using the taxation system to favour certain kinds of investments or activities. This was long the argument of social democratic theory and is still that of Keynesian or post-Keynesian liberals today. This would leave corporate power as a fundamental feature in our society, and would do nothing to redistribute wealth or bring us closer to income ratios of ten to one or five to one.

The most sensible solution, bearing in mind the kind of society we presently live in, is some form of "market socialism." Centralized planning, for all its initial successes in the industrialization of certain communist countries, has not proved a very adaptable or sophisticated system. And it has usually been the antithesis of a democratic one. Capitalist economies, for their part, have a number of technological and other successes to their credit, though failures are not lacking, as the 1980s are reminding us. The capitalist system, moreover, breeds too great a measure of inequality. This spills over into the political system as undue influence for the wealthy and impedes the realization of democracy.

"Market socialism" postulates direct ownership by the producers (not the state!) over the principal means of production. It would maintain a form of market by allowing autonomy to the economic units and competition among them. A progressive income tax system would ensure that income ratios did not exceed an agreed upon social norm.

A major attraction of "market socialism" is that it maximizes workers' participation and control (the "self-government of the producers," to use Marx's celebrated phrase). It is the workers and employees, vested with legal ownership of an enterprise or firm, who would choose its managers and board of directors, determine its major investments, and allocate any profits. A relative equality of condition would be built into the major economic units of the system, something which is a necessary precondition for political equality.

There will be further discussion of market socialism and workers' control shortly. For the moment, it is enough to underline that democratic participation in the economic sphere would require dramatic changes in the organization of our economy. I do not think that our present capitalist framework, with its concentration of power and its top-down decision making, can be adapted to the needs of a more democratic social order. If some type of participatory democracy is our goal for Canada, we must begin to envisage a post-capitalist stage of development.

IX
Base-Level Democracy

The Canadian political culture has not completely lacked grassroots traditions. The populist movements in Western Canada went deep, mobilizing large numbers of farmers and their families around the problems of the wheat economy. Political movements challenged the monopoly of the grain companies, opposed the freight policies of the railway, and pressed for low tariffs in opposition to the protectionist interests of the East. Provincial parties swept into office with ideas of delegate democracy, of recall and leadership accountability which were quite alien to the parliamentary system. The cooperative movement took hold on the Prairies, and is still important there.

The trade union movement was able to tap strong sentiment among the working class which had endured long decades of inhuman working conditions and of exploitation. Radical traditions were especially prevalent among workers in the resource sector, e.g. mining, who often lived in isolated communities. It is also worth drawing attention to the significant number of immigrants in radical working class organizations in the first half of this century. "Peace, order and good government" was demonstrably less attractive to those at the bottom of the economic and ethnic mosaic than to those at the top.

Recently the trade union movement has considerably broadened its constituency. It has achieved broader support in Quebec than it did before 1945 and it has become increasingly politicized. It has moved into the public sector across Canada, after earlier having conquered the industrial strongholds. It has increased its female component, in line with the changing roles of women workers in the economy.

Whether the trade union movement today is a grassroots organization or a bureaucratic one is another matter. Quite clearly a top-down structure prevails in many unions, as in the construction ones, with rank-and-file participation more the exception than the rule. Conversely, there is a good deal of democratic discussion and debate in many public sector unions and in a fair number of industrial ones. And the degree of mobilization that arises during strike activity or more politically defined actions—days of protest, the Common Front strike in Quebec, the Solidarity movement and strike in British Columbia—is a healthy antidote to the quiescent behaviour instilled by our political culture.

There are other multifarious movements which attest to the existence of grassroots politics. The women's movement of the last ten years is one example, despite all the attempts of the federal government to co-opt some organizations. The student movement of the 1960s was an interesting, if short-lived, example. Tenant groups, native organizations, ecology groups and the more broadly based anti-nuclear movement, gay rights groups, third world solidarity committees—the list is fortunately long. Many of these organizations have engaged in protest actions and in civil disobedience when the issues seemed of particular importance to their members. When tens of thousands of people take to the streets, as they have over the revival of the arms race or over the 'restraint' programme of the

Social Credit government in B.C., when thousands of native people or of Canadian women can be mobilized, as they were in the final stages of the constitutional debate, then the cause of political participation is not a hopeless one. Indeed, it suggests that the Canadian political culture is less uniformly parliamentary than we may have supposed.

This is good news, if we are interested in going beyond single-issue politics toward a more broadly based form of citizen democracy. For citizen democracy entails extensive grassroots participation and it can draw sustenance from the popular movements which the Canadian political culture has produced. Without romanticizing this tradition or exaggerating its strength, we should invoke it in seeking an alternative to parliamentarism.

That alternative, I have suggested, lies in some form of base-level democracy. The following proposals can not be expected to be implemented in the immediate future. But as an exercise in utopian thought, they are meant to bear some relationship to the type of society and citizenry we have today. We shall not be able to re-create the ancient polis in the late 20th century. We may, however, be able to capture something of its spirit if we think in terms that go beyond the alienating and alienated politics of our day.

The mathematics of base-level democracy revolves around something like this: The Canadian population is approaching 25 million and roughly two thirds of these are age eighteen or more. How do we provide a forum for direct participation by these 17 million or so citizens?

We must first determine what would be the maximum-sized unit which could allow face-to-face contact among its members. We do not want this number to be so small, say 100, that the total number of units would increase inordinately and make the larger scheme difficult to operate. On the other hand, we would not want a number so large, say 5000, that it would make a mockery of participation. If we recall the Athenian example, not all the citizens could be expected to attend the meetings of their base unit. We certainly do not want to coerce people into attending (that part of Rousseau we can happily drop!). Nor should we have exaggerated ideas about how high the participation would be in routine meetings of the unit. A 10 percent turn-out might be the norm, with perhaps 20-30 percent coming out for major issues, and as many as 50 percent for some annual occasion such as elections. If these approximations are close then a membership of roughly 1000 might do the trick. A gathering of 100 or less would allow for direct participation of those present. Meetings of 200-300 would be more awkward, but certainly possible to manage. Only when a meeting includes 500 or more does wide participation become impossible.

We might ask ourselves, however, whether it is likely that everyone would want to intervene in a discussion. In most gatherings, the main positions are outlined by a number of speakers. Those present then divide, once the motion has been called. This is the way things proceded in Athens and I doubt we can expect a different pattern here. We might improve on Athens by making provision for those unable (or unwilling) to attend a meeting to make their views known. We might consider the use of mail ballots or electronic ballots on substantive policy questions to ensure that the *vox populi* is heard.

But we have gotten ahead of ourselves. We were trying to determine an acceptable number of members for each unit, and 1000 seems appropriate. Not in a mechanistic way, of course. For certain rural areas this may be too large. In big cities it may be desirable to go slightly over this figure, say to 1250, to keep apartment blocks or neighbourhood areas intact.

With 17 million adult citizens and groups of about 1000 each, we would have roughly 17,000 base units in Canada.

This seems like a staggering number, even if it is broken down province-by-province. Ontario would have roughly 6000, Quebec 4000, B.C. 1700 and even little P.E.I. 75. Could such a beast ever be expected to fly?

How could the units interact with one another? How could the citizens of any one unit hope to have influence on provincial or national issues? How frequently would units meet? Who would direct the meetings and ensure that decisions were carried out? Might not a new class division arise between those who enjoy public meetings (a minority) and those who do not? The questions are legion, and I can already imagine the jaundiced reader muttering: "If this is popular sovereignty, give me Queen-in-Parliament any day." I shall have to ask such readers for their indulgence to pursue this exercise. I think it is not as quixotic as it might appear.

17,000 units would indeed be awesome, were we talking about *sovereign* entities. But none of these units is meant to be sovereign, simply to embody a fraction of what we call popular sovereignty. Representative systems have no problems establishing 50,000 or 100,000 separate polling booths for their electorates. Why should a participatory system find 17,000 unwieldy?

The internal organization of the units should not pose inordinate problems. Membership would be determined on a territorial basis, and the unit areas readjusted every five or ten years, much like parliamentary constituencies, to take account of demographic trends. One would automatically become a member of a particular base unit by residing in its area. Membership would cease on departing from it.

Each base unit could annually elect an executive committee, which would have a dual function. It would convene general meetings and would act as the contact group with other base units and outside bodies. If we wanted to follow one particular of the Athenian model, we could elect these committees by lot. This would mean that five or ten randomly chosen citizens would become the executive, not by contesting elections, but by having their names drawn from the membership list. Committee membership would change completely each year to prevent the same individuals from dominating proceedings.

How frequently should general meetings be called? One of the most telling criticisms of participatory democracy has been that people have many other pursuits: economic, familial, creative, athletic or sensual. Surely, it is argued, citizens cannot drop all their other activities to engage in nonstop political activity. Life has only so many years, and the day only so many hours.

These are valid objections. The experience of the Parisian *sections* during the French Revolution or the workers' soviets during the Russian Revolutions of 1905 and 1917 suggests that nonstop participation is extremely draining. Because of this, it rarely endures for long. In the long haul, societies must either find a way of institutionalizing and channeling participation, or see it give way to its opposite—authoritarian decision making. We could not expect a participatory system that called upon its members, week after week, to decide on all the questions of state to long survive.

So we need two things: meetings at fixed intervals, probably not more than once a month; a carefully prepared agenda which would allow discussion of a number of concerns, but not anything and everything at once.

Attending one meeting a month is not an impossible demand on the average person's time. It is a more major commitment than casting a ballot for representatives every four years, but the whole point of this exercise is to transfer some power from elected officials to the people. Participation does entail some extra involvement.

Exactly what issues would be discussed? Any member of

the base unit should have the right to propose items for the agenda. These could range from items of a strictly local or neighbourhood character, to matters touching on the municipal, regional, provincial or federal domains. They could involve decisions already made by some level of authority, laws currently up for discussion, or new proposals which citizens would like to see enacted.

Here, the role of the executive committee becomes important. Its function is to ensure that a limited number of items makes it onto any agenda, and that the issues discussed are ones which a reasonable number of citizens would consider worthwhile. Base units might circulate a monthly information sheet where proposals and opinions could be freely advanced. The agenda for each monthly meeting, however, would be the responsibility of the committee subject, of course, to the approval of the general meeting.

Let us assume that some base unit decides that a particular piece of provincial legislation—say regarding the funding of health services—is unacceptable, and passes a motion to that effect. What impact would this have? Not very much if only one unit is involved. The same would be *a fortiori* true for a piece of federal legislation.

Let us further assume, however, that there exists some liaison structure among the various base units. For example, there could be regional groupings of the base units within a municipality or other appropriate area. Each unit's executive committee could send a delegate to the meetings of these Liaison Committees. One of its functions would be to exchange information on the questions which were being discussed and on the motions passed in the different unit. This information could be brought back to each of the base units for consideration. It would be up to each base unit and its executive to decide whether a motion passed by another unit should be presented to a general meeting. In this way, a single motion might be passed by any number of base units.

This still may have no direct effect on government policy. So we may need another level of liaison. There could be an exchange of information among the different regional groupings within the province. I am not suggesting an ongoing deliberative body to usurp the powers of the legislatures; this would simply bring us back to parliamentary sovereignty under a new guise. Rather, this province-wide committee with delegates from the regional groupings would be a clearing house for the information from the units which is channelled through the regional groupings. If a motion had been passed by a fair number of units in a regional grouping it could then be brought to the attention of other groupings which might wish to take it up. (The initiative in all cases must rest squarely with the base units and their executives). With time, we might find a motion passed by a significant number of base units in a province. Even 20 percent would be significant.

In the example mentioned, this would imply a strong current of opinion against a particular piece of provincial legislation. It would suggest that the popular majority and the legislative majority may not coincide on this issue. And it would mean—if the base units were to have any real power—that such a law, unless the government put it to a province-wide referendum and it were upheld, would become null and void.

The same would hold for positive initiatives. Suppose 20 percent of the base units passed a motion calling for the shut down of nuclear power generating plants. If the provincial legislature and government refuse to comply they would be under an obligation to submit this matter to a province-wide referendum whose results would be binding.

It begins to sound as though the citizens in our participatory democracy might be voting in referenda every other week. This is highly unlikely. Any initiative, it must be remembered, must be voted and passed by a general meeting of at least 20 percent of the base units in a province. Let us use British Columbia as an example. There, 350 base units would be required to pass a motion in favour of a particular initiative before the possibility of a referendum would even arise. The executives of these base units must each have given this item an important place on the agenda of their general meetings. The citizens attending these general meetings or voting by mail or electronic ballot—in at least 350 different instances—must have decided that the matter merited their support. A referendum would only become necessary, moreover, if the provincial government then refused to go along. I doubt there would be more than a handful of cases in any one year.

The same principle could apply at the federal level. We could have a Federal Liaison Committee for the different provincial groupings. An initiative involving a federal matter passed by at least 20 percent of the base units in one province could then be brought to the attention of the base units in the other provinces. (It is likely, of course, that such information would spread through the attention of the media.) If the motion were passed by 20 percent of the base units in the whole country—some 3500—the federal government would be in the same position as just described for a provincial government. A particular law which is opposed would become null and void, unless it is upheld at a referendum. A positive initiative would automatically become law, unless the federal government opted to submit the matter to a referendum first.

A diagram might be useful to summarize the structure we have been discussing. (See following page.)

The nature of the liaison committees needs further discussion. At first glance, it looks as though I have just outlined what historians and political scientists have

Representative Structures   Base-Level Structures

Federal Government . . . . Federal Liaison Committee
(Elected Parliament)   (Delegates from Provincial
                       Liaison Committees)

Provincial Governments . . . . Provincial Liaison
(Elected Legislatures)   Committees (Delegates from
                       Municipal/Regional
                       Committees)

Municipal or Regional. . . . . . Municipal/Regional Liaison
Governments (Elected)   Committees (Delegates from
                       Base Units)

                       Base Units
                       (1000 members on average)
                       (17,000 units for Canada)

categorized as a system of "dual power." On the one hand, the elected institutions we are familiar with will continue to exist. There are periodic elections, governments are voted in and out of office, the powers of legislatures, Parliament and Cabinet appear to be the same. On the other hand, there is a parallel structure flowing from the bottom up, grounded in the principle of direct citizen participation. We have parliamentary sovereignty potentially competing with popular sovereignty. The history of dual structures, critics would suggest, is that one wins out over the other, that no long term balance can be maintained. Don't the Federal or Provincial Liaison Committees form the embryo of a parallel government?

I think not. I would underline the fact that these liaison committees are *indirectly* chosen. Their members must first be on the executives of their base units, which in turn have delegated them to serve on a Municipal/Regional Liaison Committee. This committee has in turn delegated one or more of its members to serve on the Provincial Liaison Committee. And this again has delegated members to the Federal Committee. Members of Parliament and of the legislatures, by comparison, will continue to hold a *direct* mandate from our electorate. History teaches us that greater legitimacy and power flow from direct rather than indirect election.

The memberships of the liaison committees, moreover, would rotate far more frequently than is the case in our legislative bodies. The principle of annual elections of the base-unit executives ensures that the membership of the Municipal/Regional, Provincial and Federal Liaison Committees changes completely every year. This gives a large number of ordinary citizens exposure to political responsibility. But it strongly militates against power grabbing by the committees.

Are the committees, accordingly, fated to be hollow entities? This doesn't follow either. They would cap a structure which would presumably have a high level of citizen commitment. Each base unit might have its own information and communication network. It might also liaise with economic and social institutions in its area. Regional level committees, provincial and federal ones would have their own networks. They also could have a liaison role with economic and social institutions. Nor is this all. We might want to entrust the liaison committees with control over the referendum process. It would then be their responsibility, in the event of a conflict between the base units and a level of government, to ensure that a referendum—perhaps an electronic one—was held as expeditiously as possible. Depending on the outcome, they would have the power to declare laws null and void or to decree new ones into effect—but they could never do this without the *explicit* consent of the citizens.

I don't think the system would break down. If we assume a modicum of rationality in our citizenry, they will not continuously be seeking confrontations with their elected governments. They would use their base units to influence the political process, not to stymie it. Conversely, under such a system legislatures and Parliament would be forced to pay much closer attention to the views of the ordinary citizen. They would be well aware of the current base units' discussion topics and could see the storm signals of any looming confrontation. This does not mean they would have to shelve controversial measures, but they would have to be prepared to justify them to their citizens a lot better than they do today. Isn't this a reasonable proposition in a democracy?

How much actual citizen participation should we expect? Will people really flock to these base-level assemblies? Or will power simply fall into the hands of those with a particular axe to grind? How effective a participatory democracy would it be if, for example, less than 10 percent of the citizens bothered to attend their monthly assemblies? Wouldn't it make the participation rate in parliamentary elections—an average of 70-80 percent in Canada—look good by comparison?

These are not objections I would shirk off lightly. It would be easy to retort: "Come the revolution, everything will resolve itself"; "Our new participatory citizen will inject life into all these structures"; and "A glorious tomorrow lies in front of us." But we have to be sober headed in building utopias, and realistic about the obstacles any scheme would encounter.

I implied a little earlier that I did not think political participation was *the* supreme human good. I do think it is an important human good—more so than theorists of parliamentary democracy would allow. Still, it is not meant to be the secularized incarnation of a messianic credo, sweeping everything before it.

I would not expect all the citizens in a democracy to come running to the meetings of their assemblies. The number 1000 as a talking point was based on the assumption that no more than 100 were likely to come out to an average meeting. 20-30 percent might turn out when matters of great consequence were on the agenda.

Does this spell dictatorship by the talkers over the balkers? The answer is no. First, the talkers are likely to come from all parts of the political spectrum, and are unlikely to form a cohesive political bloc. Second, those who do not come to meetings need not be penalized when important decisions have to be made. Resolutions which were to be passed on to the regional and eventually to the provincial or federal level could require a mail or electronic ballot to become valid. Not everyone is likely to vote in these either, but a majority often would. Third, if we opt for an executive chosed annually by lot, we reduce the problem of "participatory professionals" taking over the base units. Most citizens in the course of their lives will have had one year of exposure to base-level democracy from the inside—by having served on an executive committee. A good number of citizens would have acquired participatory skills. This educational function is, in fact, one of the great plusses that participatory democracy has over any purely representative system.

It isn't fair, moreover, to compare the participation rates in the monthly base-level assemblies with the turn out rates for parliamentary elections. It is more valid to compare the election figures with the participation in all the activities of the base unit over a four year period. If we assume that half the citizens will attend at least one base-unit meeting in the course of the four years, and that another 25-30 percent will mark their 'X' on some of the ballots that come their way, we really would not be doing badly. And since our model ensures that matters of real consequence come before the assemblies, these figures become quite plausible.

There are, of course, all kinds of questions that remain to be resolved. Would the members of the base units be paid for their labours, or dispensed from a certain number of hours of work? Would membership of the executive be treated like jury duty, something citizens would be unable to turn down without just cause? What sorts of budgets should the base units and liaison committees be allowed? What kind of information/communications would they produce? How would the referendum machinery work?

But these and related issues are ancillary ones. Our real concern is to determine whether the base-level idea makes sense. Is direct democracy, in a modified form, a real possibility in the modern nation-state? Could Canada, in an extraordinary break with its parliamentary traditions, be the first western country to move in that direction?

X
Market Socialism

Circumstances might not seem propitious for moving toward greater citizen participation. We are in the midst of a severe international economic crisis with the highest rates of unemployment Canada has experienced since the Great Depression. The Organization for Economic Co-operation and Development is predicting gloom and doom into the mid-1980s, and they are probably optimistic. Governments at all levels are running huge deficits, our industrial and even financial institutions are in trouble—can this be the hour for radical political reforms? We have just come through a constitutional debate in which citizen participation was, by and large, muffled. Does this suggest the existence of an aroused constituency seeking the democratization of Canadian society? Our political parties have been the privileged actors in our parliamentary system for so long. Would they not make a shambles of any scheme for direct democracy?

Yet perhaps this crisis is as good a starting point as any for the renewal of our political system. A period of crisis, unlike a period of prosperity, is a time for self-examination. It is a time in which political and economic institutions are seen to be imperfect and in need of fundamental reform. It is a time when citizens can rediscover the existence of the public sphere, and sense that the well-lived life revolves around more than material accoutrements. I think the Canadian people are waiting for something a little more compassionate than Reaganomics, a little more imaginative than warmed-over Keynesianism, something more than a Conservative government in place of a spruced-up Liberal or less-than-convincing NDP one. If I may be so bold, perhaps our polity is ripe for some radically democratic reforms.

There is nothing we can do to change our lack of a revolutionary tradition, but there is no longer any reason to live as prisoners of it. Canadians have paid a high price for the top-down style of politics (and economics) we have been saddled with. Our culture on the English Canadian side has, until recently, lacked sparkle and depth. As a tributary of Britain and the United States, it could scarcely have been different. Neither the artificial stimulation of government funding nor the passing revival of Canadian nationalism can change this entirely. A country cannot separate cultural creativity from lived history. We need more history making in this country. (Even on the Quebec side, the exhaustion of nationalism after two decades suggests the need for a new *projet collectif*.)

To make history is not necessarily to make bloody revolution. I am not calling for a storming of imaginary Winter Palaces—for barricades on the main streets of all our cities. We do need a clearer sense of what we could become as a people—if we were finally prepared to take a risk or two. A peaceful revolution would suffice, but a real one.

The present economic crisis is more than a passing recession. There is no evidence that growth and less unemployment will quickly return to the western world. There is no guarantee that the international economy will come through the decade without a major financial crisis

89

or the crumbling of the trade structures erected after Bretton Woods. How are we to cope? Canada has long had an open economy, dependent on resource exports and on the importation of both capital and manufactured goods. This may no longer be possible. Capital inflows are drying up, and our relative position in the new international division of labour is no longer so strong. Looking to the American economy to pull us out, or to the fruits of traditional monetary and fiscal stimulation, will not get us very far.

Should we expect Canadian capitalists to do the job for us? The history of big business in this country is not an appealing one. Massive land grabs and government subsidies have been one part of it. Foreign ownership and a branch-plant economy have been another. A fairly ruthless attitude toward Canadian workers and recently an increasingly rapacious posture in the third world rounds out the picture. Do we really want our economy to stay in the hands of the chartered banks, Conrad Black and his buddies in the corporate elite?

It is time we recognized that capitalism is part of the problem, not the solution. This is not to suggest that our trade or unemployment picture would magically change if we moved to another form of economy. There are structural constraints that will not go away by simply changing economic horses. What can change is our collective sense of purpose and the ties of solidarity among the producers and the workers in this country.

Suppose that overnight we decided to remove from private ownership *all* firms and enterprises which employed over 25 people or had assets in excess of $5 million. We might be prepared to offer compensation on a sliding scale, with a definite maximum—say $1 million— that any individual or family unit residing in Canada could *in toto* receive. We could also trade off the value of Canadian investments abroad for foreign assets in this country and, if necessary, throw in a little extra to pay the difference over a period of time. In other words, we would be socializing the major part of the Canadian economy. What happens now? In the short term, the Canadian dollar plunges in currency trading, the Americans roundly denounce us and put the CIA on red alert, the Europeans and the Japanese begin to wonder what cold-weather madness has come over us. We too are surprised—Canadians, after all, are not supposed to act like this. But there we are, overwhelmed by our own audacity, and forced to carry on.

Do we turn everything over to the state? This might seem like the natural recourse, in light of the role that crown corporations, federal and provincial, already play. But few Canadians would really want the state to run two thirds or three quarters of our economy. They might accept some specific state ownership, say of the banking system. They might accept a form of economic planning, with extensive consultation among the federal government, the provinces, and the different economic actors. They would, hovever, stop well short of a *state capitalist* system. (I mean by this term a system in which the state *itself* has become the overall capitalist, controlling and managing the whole economy, albeit in the name of the people. This, incidentally, is a more accurate description of the Soviet and East European economies than the labels socialist or state socialist which these regimes and their mainstream Western critics prefer. Each, for his own reasons, would like to see the concept of socialism limited to the Marxist-Leninist variants stemming from October 1917.)

Canadians, we shall assume, are capable of a little more ingenuity. You do not live for two centuries under a developed market economy to suddenly veer to the other extreme, not even if you are stuck in the middle of an economic depression. It would become evident rather quickly that something new was required. That new system, I suggested earlier, can be called "market socialism."

The newly socialized factories and enterprises would be turned over to their employees. All the employees, from managers to office clerks without distinction, would become co-owners of their enterprises. In effect, worker collectives in which each member owned one share (and no more), would become the linchpin of our economic system.

Each collective would elect a board of directors. (In larger enterprises with many branches, there would have to be local executives as well as a central board.) The board of directors would have the authority to hire management and determine policies. Salary scales would be open to extensive discussion among the rank-and-file. While significant differences would be allowed, enterprises would be legally bound not to exceed the agreed upon social norm for income differentials (e.g. five to one, or ten to one). Whenever the enterprise distributed profits among its members, each employee-shareholder would receive an equal amount. In periods of hardship such as declining markets or faltering productivity all would share equally in the reduction of revenues.

This does not mean that the collectives would *never* be able to rid themselves of redundant or undesirable members. But they would have to show cause and, in most cases, pay some remuneration. (Retiring workers might also receive something for their share in the collective and new workers pay for their share over a fixed period— something we won't worry about here.) Before any major redundancies could be decided, there would have to be a generalized discussion among the membership. Security of employment, therefore, would be a high priority.

In production or pricing policies, these enterprises would function much as capitalist enterprises do today.

Market criteria would remain important. There would, however, be a fair amount of co-ordination among different firms and industries, particularly if a system of *indicative* planning were introduced at the provincial and federal levels.

Workers' control could be partially extended to crown corporations. There is no reason that a hydro company or a radio and television network should not be managed democratically. The single notable exception might be the banking system, which would remain under direct federal (and perhaps also partly provincial) control. Control over credit would give government one important lever over the policies of the firms, something which good economic management might well require.

There are, of course, potential problems with such a scheme. There would be a fundamental inequality in the assets which different groups originally acquired. Steel workers in Cape Breton, for example, would be in a much weaker position than steel workers in the more modern plants in Hamilton. Textile workers would be at a great disadvantage compared to those working for the newly socialized Exxon or Shell.

There are no easy answers but we will have to look to national policies to reduce some of this inequality. There could be an initial evaluation of the assets of these wealthy enterprises. The worker collectives which owned them might be forced to pay a differential share of future profits to the state at higher rates than the disadvantaged. Those which had been foreign owned would also have to pay some of the compensation to the foreign owners; the same would hold true in the Canadian owned firms vis-a-vis their former owners.

The taxation system would also be available to cream off the higher incomes of better paid workers and redistribute them to the less well-off. Regional disparity programmes would be maintained and perhaps even strengthened, with the government or banks providing funds to workers in vulnerable sectors which were *worth* shoring up. But some enterprises, no doubt about it, would have to go under.

The real onus would be to develop more efficient and profitable sectors. This could be done through a combination of collective or private initiative, with state support through the banking system. In this system we, of course, have not abolished private enterprise. We are prepared to have the small entrepreneur carry on much as before. We are even prepared to finance a good deal of risk with public funds—whether of the small entrepreneur or of a group of workers. But there are limits beyond which the small entrepreneur cannot grow and still retain ownership of his or her firm. We do not want big capitalists in our society, though we will be quite happy to have small ones. So once an enterprise has grown to the limits we mentioned earlier ($5 million in assets or 25 employees), it would be turned over to the employees, with compensation of up to $1 million paid to the owner. He or she would be free to continue with the employee managed firm, albeit with no more formal power than anyone else.

With worker collectives the issue of ownership would be no problem. It would be up to the banking system to decide whether these groups had projects worth financing. (This is on the assumption that the individual members would not be able to generate the full amount of capital necessary from within the firm's profits, in the case of existing firms.) The situation would not be very different from the one that on-going enterprises seeking credit would face. Worker collectives would have to justify the viability of their projects to their creditor, which, in this case, would be owned by the state.

I can see sceptical readers shaking their heads. Doesn't this mean that the state would *de facto* be running the economy through the banks? Aren't we simply bringing in state socialism through the back door? I don't think so. First, the state itself would not, by and large, be setting up enterprises of its own. Through the banks, it would be financing ventures which individuals or employees had initiated, and for which the latter would retain responsibility and control. Second, the banks would presumably have an arm's-length relationship with governments. They would function much as crown corporations do today, with a good deal of autonomy in day-to-day decision making. This doesn't mean that governments could not develop macro-policies which the banks would follow. But that is quite a different story from a Ministry of the Plan placed in direct control of the economy. Third, while governments—federal and, I would hope, provincial—would have ultimate control over the banking system, there would also be other participants. We would want to see representatives of some of the major worker-controlled industries represented on their boards. We would want representatives from small capital. And, if our system of base-level democracy were in force, we might want to see representatives from the liaison committees as well.

There is a second major set of problems with "market socialism." How do we ensure that the employees who run industries will make wise decisions and not simply run them into the ground? What is to prevent them from gutting the firm's assets, distributing high dividends to themselves and shutting the enterprise down? How do we prevent decisions which harm the consumer, destroy the environment, or trade off long-term responsibility for short-term gain? By turning enterprises over to worker collectives in the first place, were we not hoping for a more socially responsible economic system? How do we generate a commitment to the public good?

We could draw up legal charters, making workers individually responsible for their firm's decisions—up to a certain limit. We could decree firms to be custodians of public goods, with certain responsibilities to the public, rather than the formal owners of the assets. But this sounds both too formalistic and too punitive.

We want to be sure that worker-managed industries have real incentive to place the public interest high on their agenda. The first flush of revolutionary enthusiasm may help at the beginning. Workers who suddenly find themselves in control of major enterprises will understand the chain of events which has brought this about and the significance. They will ostensibly be interested in the success of this first experiment in market socialism, and in the survival of their own firm. They will still want to have jobs which are secure five or ten years down the line, and will want the economy to generate employment for their own children. They are unlikely to want to bankrupt their firms.

Still, as critics will hasten to remind us, the worm of human greed is not easily vanquished. Somewhere, before long, a group of workers will be tempted to place short-term advantage first. Revolutionary good intentions have a way of turning sour. Market socialism will soon yield to the egoism of particular interests. Hobbes, they would argue, is a more realistic guide here than Rousseau.

Maybe. So we will be forced to think of a more enduring restraint than good intentions. What can it be? The state? We surely do not want to give the state the powers of moral custodian as well as the huge political and economic powers it already has. We know where the morality of St. Just or of Zinoviev can lead.

Who, then, could speak for the civil society and how could they influence the economic structures? Perhaps we should remember at this point the institutions we so laboriously set up in the previous section; they seemed, at first glance, to be a lot of bother, particularly when elected governments would end up making most decisions anyway.

So what if we gave our base units an additional function? They do, after all, bring together the citizens of a particular locality. In that sense, they articulate community standards better than any other institution. Why not include representation from the base units on the boards of directors of all worker-managed enterprises?

It would be quite sufficient if these directors constituted no more than 20 or 25 percent of a board. We do not want them actually controlling the firms, nor would they be much interested in all the nitty-gritty of economic decision making. These directors, however, would speak for the public interest. They would be the ones to raise environmental and consumer concerns. They could blow the whistle if it looked as though a firm were pursuing egoistical concerns, or heading down a self-destructive road.

How would such directors be named? The Regional/ Municipal Liaison Committees are probably the most appropriate bodies to make appointments for single-locality firms. The directors could be chosen from among the executives of the base units but they could also include well-known individuals in the community. Appointments might be for a two-year period to ensure that directors became familiar with the firm. These directors could receive honoraria, partly from the firms, partly out of public funds. Firms of a clearly provincial or national character could have directors appointed by the Provincial and Federal Liaison Committees.

This mechanism would strengthen the public-service component of our economic units. It would not hamper normal decision making, since the publicly appointed directors would be just as committed to the prosperity of the firm as the worker-appointed ones. But they would help to ensure that the Hobbesian impulse did not run away with our market socialist economy.

At the same time, our participatory model would draw benefits from such an arrangement. It would link the participatory institutions in the political arena with those in the economic. It would mean that citizen democracy and workers' control were not in separate airtight compartments. And it would allow civil society—not a centralized, parliamentary state nor the political parties—an important role in articulating the public good.

Whether there would still be a role for trade unions as we know them in a market socialist system, I do not know. Theoretically, with workers in control of their enterprises, able to hire and fire their managers, trade unions would be unnecessary. This, however, presupposes that there is a functioning system of workers' control in all enterprises. And it assumes that the workers' assemblies provide a democratic form of protection for workers, equal or better to what the trade unions presently provide. Workers and employees might, however, want to retain institutions distinct from the workers' councils, particularly at the provincial and national level, until the new institutions had proven themselves. We could hardly blame them.

Market socialism would have dramatic implications for a variety of sectors. With newspapers managed by their staffs, we would eliminate the monopoly chains overnight —something the Kent Commission didn't dare suggest. Staff ownership of a newspaper has worked fairly well for thirty years at *Le Monde*, arguably the world's most prestigious newspaper. This does not mean that the *Globe and Mail*, the Vancouver *Sun* or the Halifax *Chronicle* would become *Le Monde*s. But they might become lively and vital disseminators of information to their communities—far more open to the *practice* of democracy than they are today. That would be a healthy change.

Professional organizations such as hospitals or clinics, athletic organizations such as hockey teams, cultural organizations such as symphony orchestras, would change significantly under a system of self-management. This doesn't mean that competence would give way to the lowest common denominator, as the heirs of Plato are always suggesting. Competence will always be recognized —in medical or academic work, as in musical performance or athletic coaching. But what a difference to morale if all the members of these organizations had a say in how they were run. It would truly be, to cite the title of one of Christopher Hill's studies of the English Revolution, *A World Turned Upside Down*.

Nor would the state be spared a cultural revolution. We could hardly imagine worker control throughout the economy while state bureaucracies remained untouched. This does not mean that the typists in the Ministry of Finance will be doing economic forecasting along with the econometricians. (They probably could do a better job, mind you!) What it does mean is that the organization of the departments and agencies would become a good deal more participatory. While senior officials would still make final organizational decisions (and ministers the ultimate political ones), they would have to pay closer attention to the views of the lower-ranking members of their departments. There might be divisional assemblies in the Ministries, where policy matters were debated and discussed. Instead of secrecy of information, we might get some openness in our public administrations. That would be a breath of fresh air after a century of bureaucratic and ministerial privilege.

XI
Toward a New Social Contract

Worker-controlled enterprises and organizations are certainly part of any alternative which the left can propose for the corporate and statist economies under which we live. Whether these reforms would follow the lines I have sketched or some variant—such as Alec Nove's proposals in his incisive study *The Economics of Feasible Socialism*—is of moot importance. It is the logic of combining socialism with markets, economic organization with rank-and-file participation and control, that bears underlining.

Yet an abstract faith in the virtue of workplace democracy is not sufficient for the late 1980s and beyond. The experience with worker-controlled industries in Yugoslavia or, on a smaller scale, in some western countries, has not been without difficulties. This is especially true where enterprises are under-capitalized and in declining sectors, where the pressure of domestic or international competition is intense, or where, for one reason or another, the work force is less interested in the operation and viability of the enterprise than the theory would suggest.

Of more concern is the argument that de-centralized

economic structures are no substitute for national economic planning and for macro-economic policies which are designed to engender employment, sustain high productivity, and maintain adequate social services. To put all one's faith in the market side of market socialism is the equivalent of putting all one's faith in the base-level units of democracy, forgetting the need for ongoing representative structures.

At a minimum, we need to spell out more clearly what policies we might have to develop in our model economy. How would market socialism deal with the threats of structural unemployment, with the inroads of the micro-chip, with work sharing? What kind of social contract could we envisage between those who are technologically displaced or unemployable and those holding down high-paying (or, for that matter, low-paying) jobs? What kind of obligations would Canada have to other countries which are less developed and which have a less enviable position in the international division of labour?

To introduce such questions into this discussion is to remind ourselves that the post-war boom is behind us. Not only have traditional industrial sectors, such as textiles, automobiles or steel, and resource sectors like forestry or mining, come under sustained attack, but the very underpinnings of industrial society seem to be dissolving. Industrialization in the third world, multinational diversification overseas, robotization of the assembly line, and the satiation of basic consumer needs in the developed countries seem to have undermined the traditional forms of capitalist expansion. Skills, like stocks and currencies, are devalued overnight, while everywhere—even within the comfortable niches of the upper middle classes—insecurity about the future pervades the present. A fiscal crisis of the state goes hand in hand with the crisis of the capitalist system.

101

In the short term this has led to the re-emergence, in the English-speaking world at least, of an older type of economic thinking that looks back to the world of *laissez faire*. With this have come the ethics of individualism and personal success, a reaction against social expenditures and against public as opposed to private goods, and an almost bellicose support for values of authority, patriotism and social conservatism as against those of equality, participation or social justice. The policies of Margaret Thatcher, Ronald Reagan or Bill Bennett are a clear reflection of this.

But farther down the line a quite different social philosophy may be in the making. If the welfare state which post-war generations grew up in was born out of the traumas of the Depression, then a new social solidarity may yet succeed the selfishness of "the me generation." This solidarity will come with the realization that jobs will simply not be there in the numbers required for all the young people (and older ones) looking for work. It will intensify as the benefits of micro-chip technology and innovation are seen to be reserved, not for the millions whose jobs have been displaced, but for a privileged few.

Job sharing, a reduction in the work week and increased social appropriation of the benefits of the new technology lie ahead. It is impossible to contemplate a two-class society in which one class holds all the cards and the other none, at least not under the conditions of an even modestly liberal democracy. Only authoritarianism of the right—a "friendly" or less than "friendly" version of fascism— could maintain such an unequal division for any length of time.

So the call for a new social contract will become pressing. This itself might provide the impetus for us to move beyond the system of corporate domination to something different. For a mere tinkering with monetary and fiscal policy would be insufficient to allay so explosive a set of contradictions.

It is precisely at such a juncture that market socialism might become attractive. How would it affect the distribution of jobs and income? And what role would we expect governments to play in ensuring that this distribution is socially acceptable?

It has been suggested that worker-controlled enterprises would have a stronger incentive to retain jobs for their members than capitalist firms presently do for their employees. But there are limits to what even such enterprises could do, faced with decreasing demand for their products and services or with competing technologies. And without significant financial or social incentives, the likelihood of their members opting for work-sharing schemes would be lessened.

The economic role of government under market socialism would include the maximization of socially useful employment, whether or not this fell within such traditional employment sectors as resources and manufacturing. It would also entail a form of social contract in which social rewards were allocated to all *active* members of society, whether engaged in "productive" or "nonproductive" activities in the classic economic sense.

Economic policy could be framed to favour work-sharing schemes over traditional work-week employment. The hours of the working week could be adjusted upward or downward to correspond to the time necessary to produce the required goods and services. Various community-related projects could be launched and funded through general revenues (and a genuinely progressive taxation system), providing alternative employment opportunities for hundreds of thousands of Canadians. A significant amount of socially relevant employment could also be generated if we paid those who performed executive functions in base-unit and liaison committees.

Community projects would not be the exclusive

103

responsibility of the central or provincial governments. We could give liaison committees a role in initiating, vetting and approving such projects, within financial guidelines set by governments.

What government policies would do is shift social priorities from an essentially "productivist" and individual focus to a more "consumptionist" and collective one, from the world of the private person to that of the public. Under market socialism, most people would work in worker-controlled enterprises or community projects and activities. All citizens, moreover, would belong to the network of base units and liaison committees. Therefore, a bias toward public goods would not automatically translate into an aggrandizement of the state or the absorption of civil society into the state. There would be sufficient de-centralization of both political and economic power to prevent this.

At the same time, new bonds of solidarity would be forged within the different sectors of the economy and within the communities and regions, more powerful than the bonds which we have. Out of such solidarities a stronger national solidarity would form and a genuinely popular basis for sovereignty would develop.

This may seem the most far-fetched proposition of all, presupposing some kind of change in human nature from a selfish to a more solidaristic pole. And it may seem less than evident that the solidarity forged around a particular work place, community, gender, or ethnic group would translate into wider solidarity. But when one remembers how *unnatural* the capitalist ethic was when it developed in the 17th and 18th centuries and supplanted long-established patterns of solidarity, we may be allowed to hazard such a proposition. There is nothing *per se* unnatural about human solidarity, once the props of capitalist interest have been weakened. Individual and group conflicts would not disappear, but a major transformation in economic structures could not but affect mentalities and collective behaviour. Particularly so since there is already a widespread sense of the moral emptiness of capitalism abroad—for all the desperate attempts by its apologists to convince us otherwise. We greatly underestimate the human capacity, if not for altruistic action, then at least for more cooperative conduct. So much the positive lessons coming out of most of the 20th-century revolutions, from China to Nicaragua, can teach us.

There would be a more powerful incentive to pursue international solidarity as well. The weakening ties between the Canadian and American economies, which a full-blooded scheme of market socialism would entail, could significantly disrupt the traditional Canadian-American trade pattern. While we could hardly find instant replacement markets in Europe, Japan or the third world, we would be forced to diversify our external economic ties.

Canadians would discover that we are not on a North American island unto ourselves and that life is just as possible with less of Uncle Sam as it was when the British connection was sundered. Third options in our foreign policy would leave the realm of the drawing board and the academic round table, as nationalism went hand-in-hand with an opening to the outside world. We might become more sensitive to third world concerns about the biases of the IMF and the World Bank and we might support the call for a fairer and more equitable distribution of goods internationally. Market socialism just might make better international citizens of us all.

These speculations are not meant to be the definitive treatment of the subject. I can hardly claim to have presented a fully worked-out model of market socialism, and I have opened myself to counterattacks. Still, there is little to be gained from fighting the familiar economic battles: the state vs. the private sector; Keynesianism vs.

mónetarism, or even foreign ownership vs. Canadian.

The choice we face is not simply between capitalism and the mixed economy on the one hand and Marxist-Leninist statism on the other. There are alternative social philosophies; there are better ways of organizing our economic activities and giving them a sense of common purpose. Any self-respecting country owes itself at least one wild fling during the course of its collective life. Why not market socialism?

XII
The Legend of the Lawgiver

At first glance, it may seem like an impossibly long road from the theory of base-level democracy or market socialism to the realities that face us. It may also seem that what began as a critique of parliamentary sovereignty has taken me in rather incongruous directions. Is the author really serious in suggesting popular sovereignty to his compatriots? Has he not allowed his pique about Canadian history and the constitution to entrap him in chimerical proposals?

I began this essay by arguing that no country in the modern world has developed a fully functioning model of democracy. Liberal democracies, by and large, are content to reduce the role of the citizen to voting for competing political candidates. "Actually existing socialisms," i.e. the Soviet Union and its allies, argue that citizen democracy flourishes under a one-party state which, unlike its capitalist competitors, speaks for the interests of working people. Their structures are so hierarchical, however, and so impermeable to grassroots control (other than through revolt) as to suggest what the Greek political thinkers called "the perversion of a good regime." In the third world, the legacy of imperialism is so present, the economic and demographic problems so acute, the political structures so fragile, to render citizen democracy a far-off ideal.

I could fend off critics by invoking the poetic licence given to any theorist—the right to spin webs from his imagination. What matters it to me if my proposals are practical or not? As long as this reading of democracy seems cogent, I am justified in directing my fire at the money-changers in our midst. I can develop schemes for greater citizen democracy in Canada, oblivious to what the political market will or will not bear. I am not running for public office; I am not a speech writer for any political leader; I am not an editorialist for a Thomson or a Southam newspaper. I can speak freely, with all the rights that the 1/25,000,000th of sovereignty vested in me (and *not in some Queen-in-Parliament*) allows.

Deep down, I might find this a romantic posture to adopt. I would have done my duty, followed a call from the political wilderness, a little like the Leveller tract, *Jonah's Cry out of the Whale's Belly*. My academic readers could say "Tut, tut" or "Very nice" and go back to monitoring parliamentary elections or to plotting the trajectory of demand curves. My one or two readers from the corporate sector or from the trade union movement would say "How weird!" and file the essay in the drawer for crack-pots, the one once reserved for Henry George, Thorstein Veblen, and Major Douglas. And the *literati*, always on the search for something novel, would give my essay a condescending pat or two and get on with plumbing the neuroses in the Canadian psyche.

An inner voice would gnaw at me before long. "Resnick, you're not going to let the bastards off the hook that easily. You owe it to yourself, to your fellow sovereign citizens, to develop your arguments a little further, to show that they are not the ravings of a theory-crazed loony." And sure enough, I would return to the fray, determined to show that my analysis of Canadian political culture and of how it might be democratized were meant as serious propositions.

One last allegory might now be in order. This one would have to be my own.

The Legend of the Lawgiver

Imagine a mythical lawgiver come to a land in the midst of a great famine. The rich have hoarded the grain and corn in silos, and keep these under armed guard night and day. The poor pray to the king and to their gods for succour, but nothing comes.

A plague breaks out in the slums of the capital city and spreads, street by street, to the palaces and villas of the rich. Death, the great equalizer, mows down rich and poor, leaving only a bare handful—one in ten or one in 100—to carry on. What will this lawgiver decide?

The rich insist that the old regime, king and all, must be restored. Many may have died, but now, in the midst of famine and plague, is no time for experiments. The poor insist that the guilty be punished for their avarice. Moreover, all grain from this time forth should belong in the public domain.

The lawgiver, a stranger from across the seas with flowing robes and beard (but others claim a woman, with cascading hair to her waist), listens carefully to both arguments. Then he (or she) takes a bag of grain, scattering the seeds to the four winds, and cries out: "Who will gather the seeds before dark?" The people run off in all directions. By evening all have a pile, small or large, to bring to the elevated hill at the outskirts of the city.

But the lawgiver has disappeared. He (or she) has left a scroll in symbols that no one can decipher, and the outlines of the state's boundaries on a parchment map. The rest is blank. For three nights and days the people debate this strange apparition. And then the grain begins to sprout, until the plains are covered with green shoots, and the wheat lies thick.

Each year, from that time on, the people gather at the site to celebrate the passage of the lawgiver. And each time they spend three nights and days debating the scroll the stranger left behind, and retelling the events that brought him (or her) to their stricken land.

Thus, the first citizen assemblies came to the earth.

We do not live in the age of mythical lawgivers. The ones we have—self-annointed by and large—do not bequeath us allegorical scrolls which *we* can then fill out. They prefer to spell out, with varying degrees of detail, the powers vested in the compartments of the state, and to reserve to themselves, or to their parliamentary assemblies, the sovereign power.

My purpose in writing this essay has been straight-forward. It is not to develop a fully worked-out blueprint for attaining direct democracy in Canada. Nor is it to definitively nail my banner to the masts of market socialism. Each of these would require a longer and more detailed exposition.

What is important is to stimulate discussion in this country. Our political culture has hitherto been remarkably impervious to political ideas. The labels "conservative" and "liberal," which we give to the two major political parties, have always been meaningless; neither one has ever been a party of ideas. The Conservatives were for long the British party; the Liberals for much of this century were the American one. In their domestic policies, it would have taken a veritable Diogenes to discover where the differences between the two lay. Each stood foursquare behind the "free enterprise" system; each was prepared to use the state as an instrument of public policy; each has used repression—the Conservatives at Winnipeg in 1919, the Liberals in Quebec in October 1970; each introduced reforms—Macdonald his Trade Union legislation of 1872 and R.B. Bennett his New Deal measures, the Liberals a variety of social programmes since World War II such as the Canada Pension Plan and Medicare.

Some might find great virtue in the fact that ideas have not enjoyed a more honoured place in the Canadian political culture. "Look at other countries," they might argue, "that have placed ideas first. Do we really want the totalitarianisms of the right and left, the fanatics of religious revivalism and nationalist excess?" They would happily retreat to the comforts of parliamentary tradition, and to parties that elevate pragmatism to the highest political art.

I have not claimed in this essay that Canada is a particularly oppressive country to live in. (Though our native people, many of our immigrants and our poor, and some Quebec nationalists might have less charitable things to say.) Nor am I so enamoured of political ideas that I am prepared to blindly embrace any ideological system that comes along.

There is, however, no special virtue in *spurning* political ideas. It does make a world of difference if those ideas are democratic or not, if they seem to open the door to worthwhile political change, if they provide the citizens with goals which make the polity come alive in a humanly enriching way. I am using loaded terms: "democratic," "worthwhile," "humanly enriching"; but political theory, by definition, is a normative enterprise. Why can we not harness it to generate a more participatory polity?

The pragmatism of our political culture has been more a curse than a blessing. Like the common law tradition, it imposes itself from precedent to precedent, with a tyranny all its own. We never get out from under the eternal federal-provincial debates, the fudging of other issues, the excessive personalization of political dialogue. We are

111

reduced to building political philosophy out of nothing more substantial than federalist doctrine and regionalist or nationalist aspirations. Party programmes read like mail-order catalogues—style and packaging more important than contents. Day-to-day politics hinge on Prime Minister X's whims and Premier Y's fancies. Canadian politics is as boring and as predictable as Canadian history.

"It ain't necessarily so," or it needn't be so, if we could somehow break the stranglehold that parliamentary politics has exercised for so long. The ordinary citizen is quite capable of exercising his or her judgement on most matters of public concern. Few, of course, will have the time to go into all the details a particular government policy may entail. Nor will all be equally interested or affected by all measures. But politics is not a kingly art; we must find a way to bring it into the reach of the ordinary citizen.

Our political culture would come alive if this occurred. Base-level democracy would make politics cease to be a spectator sport. It would remove the monopoly of political power from elected politicians and spread some of it to every assembly of citizens in the country. It would give us that rootedness in something larger which, at its best, was the glory of the ancient city-state.

But how do we get there? What scenario would make any sense in our present situation? What instruments lie at hand that could help move us toward a more participatory and egalitarian society?

I have to be realistic. There is no magic wand that any one can wave, no Moses waiting to lead us to a promised land. If we are to make such a journey it will be without a lawgiver. It will be because tens and hundreds of thousands of Canadians begin to question the system we now have, begin to think in terms of an alternative. It will be because some of the ideas I have been discussing, and

112

others as well, may make more sense in the Canada of the late 1980s than ever before.

For all the crises in capitalism today, we remain a rich country, one of the wealthiest in the world. We have a population which, by the standard of the modern nation-state, is not too large. We have a relatively tolerant political tradition—the good side of our liberal past. We have a high level of literacy and skill among our citizens, and well-developed media and communications systems. We are *anything but* the wretched of the earth, much as we share a responsibility toward them.

Citizen democracy does not easily develop under conditions of deprivation and squalor. It does not flourish where political liberties are denied. It does not have pride of place in societies where the cult of industrialization and economic accumulation comes first.

There may come a stage in history when scarcity—in its primitive sense—has been overcome. Food and shelter and the basic material things of life are then no longer the burning problems. If anything, there is then a spiritual thirst, which all the material accumulations fail to satisfy.

I think we have reached such a stage in Canada and, indeed, in other advanced capitalist countries. I do not want to call it the affluent society; this makes light of the very real inequalities and hardships that remain. But the term "post-scarcity society" does seem to describe it, at least for the majority of our inhabitants.

One of the features of a post-scarcity society is the search for some higher set of public goods than existed before. This helps explain the accelerated take-off of the welfare state in the post-World War II period, the appearance of new environmental movements in the 1970s, the increased concern about nuclear weapons today. It goes hand in hand with the questioning of conventional authority in other areas as well—science or medicine, education or the corporate sector.

A move from representative forms of democracy to a more participatory polity may be in the cards. We have seen hints of this in the wave of referenda held across North America in the early 1980s to freeze the arms race. Such referenda, of course, had no binding power. But perhaps this will not remain the case.

As the working week grows shorter, as job sharing spreads with the intensification of the economic crisis, the amount of time that people have for political concerns will grow. And the desire for political commitments, to something larger than the immediate sphere of the family, friends or work companions, will grow too. Alienation in advanced capitalist societies is as much a political as an economic phenomenon. People are increasingly searching for a form of political community to redress the powerlessness they experience vis-a-vis governments—national and regional.

People, by and large, do not find such a community in the traditional political party. This is the real reason that membership in political parties, of the left no less than of the right, has been declining in recent decades. This is not to suggest that electoral politics is irrelevant. We have seen a fair number of instances in recent years where elections have clearly been of consequence—Thatcher or Reagan or Bennett on the one hand, Mitterand, Papandreou or Gonzalez on the other. But electoral politics remains *up there* and leaves a great deal wanting.

So the search will continue for something beyond the parliamentary, in Canada as in other Western countries. We just may be in a more fortunate position to make this jump; we do have certain advantages, which I've mentioned. There is one other factor, institutional this time, that could weigh in the balance.

Hitherto, I have not said much about federalism. There have been passing references to it in the discussion of the constitution. And in the section on base-level democracy, I

114

implied there would be provincial, no less than federal, structures.

Federalism has been a negative force in this country in several respects. It has distorted our political agenda and made the tug-of-war between Ottawa and the provinces seem to be the Prime Mover. "Creative politics," to use John Porter's expression, has too often gone by the boards. Federalism, moreover, meant that Canadians were saddled with provincial regimes which were ill-equipped to deal with the problems—from resource management to social policy—of the 20th century. Nor should we forget the leverage which big business, foreign and Canadian, acquired by being able to play off one level of government against another.

Still, I am not one of those on the left who thinks that federalism is inherently a wicked thing. There have been certain advantages to the division of authority as we know it in this country. First, it has allowed people a greater affinity with their governments than would have been possible in a strictly centralized state. Democracy *can* be advanced when a large political community is broken down into smaller units. This is by no means always the case, as the examples of Duplessis, Hepburn or W.A.C. Bennett attest. But it remains a genuine possibility under federalism. Second, the federal structure did allow Quebec to survive as a distinct national community, albeit not an independent one. I think Canada has gained enormously from the existence of two major national groupings and I would not necessarily have preferred the European-style nation-state—even if the price has sometimes been a less effective central government. Third, the existence of federal units does allow for a measure of experimentation which unitary states lack. Thus, a province like Saskatchewan could pioneer medicare, which was then picked up and developed across the country. Ontario could introduce publicly owned hydro, which was gradually

115

copied elsewhere. This is important when we are talking about institutional innovations like base-level democracy.

It may be too much to expect the whole of Canada to go the route I have outlined in my discussion of base-level democracy. The 1960s are behind us; I will not, to use a phrase from May 1968, "Take my desires to be reality." A country as cautious in its political ways as ours will not suddenly undertake Olympic slaloms.

But why could some such reform not be introduced into one of the provinces? Even this may seem a daydream, albeit less so than the larger one. But if we remember the tradition of grassroots democracy that has flourished in Western Canada, it becomes slightly more plausible. For base-level democracy is, in a sense, a more developed version of what Prairie and Western populism were all about.

We would need to win a political party over to the cause. I don't think starting a *Base-Level Democracy Party* or *People's Party* or *Solidarity Party* would get us very far. My hunch is that the NDP, at least at the provincial level, is a viable possibility.

The federal New Democratic Party is as parliamentary in composition and nature as the Liberals and Conservatives—possibly even more so. Fabian socialism, with its undiluted faith in reform through Parliament, has left a lasting mark. The legacy of F.R. Scott, the League for Social Reconstruction and David Lewis stalks the corridors of the federal caucus. We saw this all too well during the Constitutional Debate.

But provincially, especially in Western Canada, the NDP is a more populist party. There have already been one or two reforms toward participation by provincial NDP governments. Saskatchewan with its community clinics, British Columbia with its Human Resource Boards, are two examples which spring to mind. Is it idle speculation to suggest that one of the provincial NDPs in

116

Western Canada might introduce a version of base-level democracy?

(It is also possible that the Parti Quebecois, now that sovereignty-association is in shambles, will look for something different to offer the electorate. But I suspect base-level democracy would be tried in Western Canada first, once the current neo-conservative wave has exhausted itself.)

Market socialism, it goes without saying, could not be introduced into one province alone. So fundamental a change in the structure of our capitalist economy would require federal action. Base-unit democracy, insofar as municipal/regional or provincial matters are concerned, is another story. This is within the purview of the provinces to enact. Moreover, the base units, once established, might press for discussion of federal concerns. There would be some spill-over from this into the federal arena, while the pressure grew for a through *aggiornomento* of our political system.

All this is for the benefit of those readers who would accuse me of hopeless impracticality. Invoking federalism is no guarantee that any province will actually choose to go this route. It merely moves the whole scheme a little closer to the realm of the possible.

We cannot yet answer the question of whether popular, as opposed to parliamentary, sovereignty can actually make it onto our political agenda. This requires far more than one author or one essay can offer. Still, I would be pleased if this little volume helped, in a modest way, to bring such matters up for wider discussion. Heaven knows, our political culture could do with some renewal. And it would be nice to believe that *The Legend of the Lawgiver* was an allegory *for our times.*

Bibliography

A list of some of the articles and books which are referred to in the essay or which touch upon themes I have discussed.

Aitken, H.G.J., "Defensive Expansionism: The State and Economic Growth in Canada," *Approaches to Canadian Economic History*, W.T. Easterbrook and M.H. Watkins, eds., Carleton Library Number 31.

Anderson, Perry, "Origins of the Present Crisis," *New Left Review*, No. 23.

Bercuson, David and McNaught, Kenneth, *The Winnipeg Strike: 1919,* Toronto, 1974.

Brus, W., *The Market in a Socialist Economy*, London, 1972.

Canovan, Margaret, *Populism*, New York, 1981.

Carnoy, Martin and Shearer, Derek, *Economic Democracy: The Challenge of the 1980s*, New York, 1980.

Corry, J.A., *The Growth of Government Activities since Confederation*, Study for the Royal Commission on Dominion-Provincial Relations, 1939.

Dahl, Robert, *After the Revolution*, New Haven, 1970.

Dahl, Robert, *Dilemmas of Pluralist Democracy*, New Haven, 1982.

Ehrenberg, Victor, *The Greek State*, London, 1974.

The Federalist Papers, especially numbers 10, 39, 48, 51, 63.

Gorz, Andre, *Les chemins du paradis*, Paris, 1983.

118

Grant, George, *Lament for a Nation*, Carleton Library, Number 50.

Hardin, Herschel, *A Nation Unaware*, Vancouver, 1974.

Hirschman, Albert O., *The Passions and the Interests: Political Arguments for Capitalism before its Triumph*, Princeton, 1977.

Hirschman, Albert O., *Shifting Involvements: Private Interest and Public Action*, Princeton, 1982.

Innis, Harold, *Essays in Canadian Economic History*, Toronto, 1956.

Jones, A.H.M., *Athenian Democracy*, Oxford, 1960.

"The Laxer Report," *Canadian Forum*, February 1984, 7-16.

Macpherson, C.B., *The Life and Times of Liberal Democracy*, Oxford, 1977.

Macpherson, C.B., *The Political Theory of Possessive Individualism*, Oxford, 1962.

Mansbridge, Jane, *Beyond Adversary Democracy*, New York, 1980.

Marx, Karl, *The Civil War in France.*

Michels, Robert, *Political Parties*, The Free Press, Glencoe, 1958.

Mill, James, *An Essay on Government*, Cambridge, 1937.

Mill, John Stuart, *Representative Government*, Everyman's Library, London, 1968.

Niosi, Jorge, *Canadian Capitalism*, Toronto, 1981.

Nove, Alec, *The Economics of Feasible Socialism*, London, 1983.

Pateman, Carole, *Participation and Democratic Theory*, Cambridge, 1970.

Plato, *The Protagoras.*

Richards, John, "Populism: A Qualified Defence," *Studies in Political Economy*, Spring, 1981.

Rousseau, J.J., *Considerations on the Government of Poland.*

Rousseau, J.J., *The Social Contract.*

Ryerson, Stanley, *Unequal Union*, Toronto, 1968.

Schumpeter, Joseph, *Capitalism, Socialism and Democracy,* 3rd edition, New York, 1950.

Siegfried, Andre, *The Race Question in Canada*, Carleton Library, No. 29.

119

Thompson, E.P., "The Peculiarities of the English," *The Poverty of Theory and Other Essays*, New York, 1978.
Vanek, Jaroslav, ed., *Self-management: Economic Liberation of Man*, Penguin, 1975.
Walzer, Michael, "A Day in the Life of a Socialist Citizen," *Radical Principles*, New York, Basic Books, 1980.
Whitaker, Reg, "Images of the State in Canada" in Leo Panitch, *The Canadian State*, Toronto, 1977.